STANDARD DOCUMENTS
FOR
COMMUNITY DEVELOPMENT
VENTURE CAPITAL TRANSACTIONS

Joseph W. Bartlett
David Ehrenfest Steinglass

Community Development Venture Capital Alliance
and
University Press of America,® Inc.
Lanham • New York • Oxford

Copyright © 1998 by
University Press of America,® Inc.
4720 Boston Way
Lanham, Maryland 20706

12 Hid's Copse Rd.
Cummor Hill, Oxford OX2 9JJ

Library of Congress Cataloging-in-Publication Data

Bartlett, Joseph W.-
Standard documents for community development venture capital transactions /
Joseph W. Bartlett, David Ehrenfest Steinglass.
p.   cm.

1. Venture capital—Law and legislation—United States. 2. Community development—
Law and legislation—United States. I. Steinglass, David Ehrenfest. II. Title.
KF1380.5.B37   1997   346.73'0682—dc21   97-41244 CIP

ISBN 0-7618-0953-8 (cloth: alk. ppr.)
ISBN 0-7618-2090-6 (pbk: alk. ppr.)

⊖™ The paper used in this publication meets the minimum
requirements of American National Standard for Information
Sciences—Permanence of Paper for Printed Library Materials,
ANSI Z39.48—1984

TABLE OF CONTENTS

Social Covenants: A Survey of the Investment Agreements of
Five Community Development Venture Capital Funds

CDVCA Standard Documentation Project
Preface

The world of community development finance has grown increasingly sophisticated in its multi-faceted responses to poverty, joblessness and environmental degradation. One of the most sophisticated approaches yet involves the marriage of the tools of venture capital and private equity investing with a wide range of social goals. This approach--what is termed by its adherents "community development venture capital"--has been successful at stimulating productive economic activity in resource-starved communities while encouraging the creation and growth of businesses dedicated to the "double bottom line."

The authors of this volume became involved with community development venture capital, one as a master practitioner and the other as a student of venture capital law, because of a shared interest in using the tools of the private equity world to address some of the problems of the broader world in which we live. We were asked to adapt the model documents found in Joe Bartlett's *Equity Finance* treatise for use by a coalition of funds engaged in a different kind of private equity investing. Throughout the process of adaptation, we came to realize that the differences were less significant than the similarities. As a result, the documents in this volume (a small sample of the larger range of documents found in the treatise) depart less than we thought they might from standard "deal" documents from a private equity transaction.

As such, they may be equally useful for anyone entering into a private equity transaction. At the very least, they provide a road map of issues of which one should be aware in making a private equity investment (or in soliciting one). Copies of these documents are available on diskette for IBM-compatible computers running Microsoft Word 3.0 or higher. If you are interested contact CDVCA at the address in the Introduction.

A word of caution: Every transaction is unique. The laws of each state differ. These documents are derived from a variety of transactions over the course of decades. Although they represent the lessons of those years of experience, they should not be used as—and *are not intended to be*—a substitute for the advice of a lawyer familiar with your specific transaction and the state laws that govern that transaction. They are also more helpful if read in conjunction with the treatise to which they constantly refer. Information on how to buy the treatise follows.

Joseph W. Bartlett, Esq.
David Ehrenfest Steinglass, Esq.
New York City, April, 1997

Joseph W. Bartlett

Joseph W. Bartlett is a partner at Morrison & Foerster, LLP in the firm's New York City office. He is also an adjunct professor at New York University School of Law. Mr. Bartlett is an expert in, among other things, corporate restructurings and venture capital transactions.

He has published numerous articles and books including: *Equity Finance: Venture Capital, Buyouts, Restructurings and Reorganizations*, (Wiley 1995, Supp. 1996, 1997); *Corporate Restructurings: Reorganizations and Buyouts*, (Wiley 1991; Supp. 1992, 1993); *Venture Capital: Law, Business Strategies and Investment Planning*, (Wiley 1989; Supps. 1990, 1991, 1992, 1993, 1994) and *The Law Business: A Tired Monopoly* (Rothman, 1982). Mr. Bartlett "literally wrote the book on venture capital financing."[1]

A former Undersecretary of Commerce, law clerk to Chief Justice Earl Warren and President of the Boston Bar Association, Mr. Bartlett graduated from Stanford Law School where he was president of the *Law Review*. He has been an acting professor of law at Stanford and an instructor in law at Boston University Law School. Mr. Bartlett has been profiled in trade publications as one of the leading practitioners in venture capital nationwide.

Mr. Bartlett has acted as counsel to, a director of, and shareholder in, a number of development stage companies during his 35 year career in the venture capital business. He was a founding stockholder and a director of GMIS, Inc.; chairman of a publicly traded REIT. Mr. Bartlett has been a director of, among others, Advanced Telecommunications Corp.; Shawmut Bank N.A.; the Shawmut Corporation; the Harbor National Bank; and the Northeast Federal Savings and Loan Association. He has served as a trustee of a series of public mutual funds and as counsel to asset managers throughout his career, including the managers of public and privately invested assets. He has a been a limited partner in a number of pooled investment vehicles, including Bain Capital and Needham Emerging Growth Partners.

Mr. Bartlett is a member of the Council on Foreign Relations, a member of the Board of Trustees and Finance Committee of Montefiore Medical Center and Director of Cyrk, Inc.

---

[1] Woolsey, "The In Between: Venture Capital Lawyers Pair Investors with Entrepreneurs," *Business Law Today* 14 (Nov/Dec 1996).

AN INTRODUCTION TO COMMUNITY DEVELOPMENT VENTURE CAPITAL

Few areas of enterprise seem more fundamentally at odds: *community development,* with subsidized programs attempting to reduce poverty in disadvantaged regions, and *venture capital,* with investment partnerships concentrating on high-growth, high-tech start-up companies.

These differences are manifest in many ways. Community development initiatives are organized through small, local nonprofit organizations, supported by charitable contributions, grants and concessionary loans. Venture capital is funded through large, national limited partnerships, capitalized by institutional investors seeking a substantial premium over the return yielded by other asset classes.

THE COMMUNITY DEVELOPMENT VENTURE CAPITAL ALLIANCE (CDVCA) is an association of venture capital funds, community development corporations and others who recognize that these two pursuits - community development and venture capital - can and should be brought together in powerful new ways.

A NEW KIND OF VENTURE CAPITAL

CDVCA members represent a new breed of venture capital, one that addresses head on some of the fundamental social and environmental questions that underlie the venture capital process:

Is it possible for companies to balance the needs of their communities with the imperatives of distant shareholders and financial markets? - What happens to employees, customers, communities and ecosystems when entrepreneurs maximize growth in pursuit of a public stock offering? Is "environmentalism" something that small companies and job-starved communities can afford?

Such questions are generally viewed by investors as externalities, factors which might reduce the rate of return to their portfolios.

The essence of venture capital lies between:

- Providing capital and management assistance to companies creating innovative solutions to social and environmental problems; and
- Institutional investors placing bets on potential $1 billion technologies.

1

CDVCA members integrate community and environmental concerns into professionally managed venture capital portfolios.

Community development venture capitalists seek to expand the vernacular of their trade from "home runs," "early ripening lemons" and "walking wounded" to include "corporate citizenship," "sustainability" and "social entrepreneurship." They do so in collaboration with the growing number of talented entrepreneurs who share such concerns. And they do so while building diversified portfolios of small, attractively priced venture investments.

WHY "COMMUNITY DEVELOPMENT VENTURE CAPITAL?"

Community development financial institutions pursue a range of lending strategies, including housing loans, credit unions and loan funds, micro-loan programs, and small business lending and technical assistance, but their development initiatives have generally not included equity investments in early-stage companies. Nevertheless, dynamic forces drive the need and the opportunity for community development venture capital.

First, it has become increasingly clear that debt alone cannot service many of the companies at the base of sound local economies. Fledgling companies need patient capital to grow.

At the same time, tens of thousands of promising new companies every year fall through the investment screen of traditional venture capital funds, which are oriented toward a small group of high-technology companies with special potential for growth.

Finally, a number of mature community development corporations and small, development-oriented venture funds - each funded independently responding to local needs - are beginning to see themselves as part of an evolving national infrastructure of human resources and local business knowledge. They are in a unique position to make small-scale equity investments in private companies in their regions.

MISSION

Members of CDVCA each pursue aspects of the following broad mission:
- To promote creation of jobs and wealth among economically disadvantaged populations and regions;
- To provide entrepreneurial solutions to social and environmental problems;
- To be a constructive influence on the formation and culture of young companies with respect to equity, sustainable community development and environmental impact; and
- To generate long-term capital appreciation.

The CDVCA was formed in 1994 to assist its members in a variety of ways. Because community development venture capital funds are typically small, young and often far from major markets, providing access to information and technical assistance are core CDVCA services.

CDVCA IS ORGANIZED TO:

- Collect and present industry data, assist members in exchanging information and sharing experience, develop case studies and arrange one or more meetings each year for CDVCA members;
- Interface with other community development financial institutions and traditional venture capital groups; and
- Track policy and funding trends, including federal legislation, economically targeted investing programs, the Community Reinvestment Act and Small Business Administration programs.

WHAT KIND OF COMPANIES?

While coinvestment with traditional venture firms occurs on occasion, the portfolio companies of most CDVCA members generally are distinguished from those of traditional venture capital funds by virtue of size, stage or other factors. For example, consider the actual experience of two companies raising venture capital:

Company A is a neuroscience start-up, with world-class scientists conducting research and development for Alzheimer's and Parkinson's pharmaceuticals. It sought $20 million in venture capital and its business plan showed no sales within five years.

Company B, located one mile away in a major metropolitan area, provides alternative site mental health services, has been in business for more than five years, and grew on $10,000 of founder's equity and $300,000 of bank debt to $6.5 million in sales. Its business is low-margin and nonproprietary, but is provides cost-effective, high-quality, innovative services to a large, predictable market. It sought $750,000 to grow over five years to sales of $15 million.

Company A raised its capital in a few months, at a valuation approaching $40 million. Company B needed almost a year to raise its capital, at a valuation of less than $3 million. Company B reached $14 million in sales in three years and was acquired by a public company, tripling its venture capitalists' investments.

As the venture capital industry has matured over the past 15 years, funds have become larger and skewed toward later stage investments. Capital under management per venture firm is measured in hundreds of millions. "The result, some say, is a paradox," wrote one analyst. "Venture capitalists have more money than ever before but start-ups find it harder to find backing."[*]

---

[*] N.Y. Times, Oct. 8, 1989, "Venture Capital Loses Its Vigor."

The venture capital industry invests roughly $2.5 billion each year in 1,000 companies or less; 500,000 companies or more start up each year. Of the companies that do receive venture capital, a large percentage are later stage, expansions or leveraged buyouts.

CDVCA members are interested in the tens of thousands of start-ups and early stage companies that have reasonable growth potential but still far short of the threshold of the larger venture capital funds. Consider the following examples of current CDVCA member portfolio companies:

Natural Chemistry, Inc.

New Canaan, CT - A developer of enzyme-based cleaners and additives for swimming pools and spas, the company is rapidly achieving national distribution and penetrating major accounts. Founded in 1992, the company expects to reach $10 million in sales by 1998.

Intelligent Controls, Inc.

Saco, ME - A manufacturer and marketer of leak detection systems for underground storage tanks. The company passed $7 million in sales in 1994 and was listed on the American Stock Exchange in earlier 1995.

DataBeam

Lexington, KY - The company provides software for multiple location white board conferencing. Databeam has recently licensed its software to Microsoft for inclusion into the DOS operating system.

Larex International, Inc.

Hibbing, MN - The company has developed a highly efficient process for extracting and refining a specific type of sugar present in small concentrates in all plants and animals, but present in fairly large concentrations in a specific species. The sugar has a broad array of uses at various levels of refinement. The company will be constructing its manufacturing facility in 1995, and anticipates rapid sales growth.

THE FUTURE OF CDVCA

CDVCA members face many challenges and opportunities. Questions of scale, liquidity and rate of return remain central. Members share a responsibility to measure performance and refine their understanding of the risk/return characteristics of community development venture capital.

In coming decades, community, environmental and financial factors will increasingly converge, driven not only by advocacy, but also by consumer and investor demand. Community development venture capital will plan an important role in this process.

By bringing new tools to existing community development organizations, the CDVCA can provide an important vehicle for their strategic growth and capital formation. By making equity capital available to entrepreneurs in economically disadvantaged areas, we can support the building of local economies. By deploying venture capital at a smaller scale, we can affirmatively shape the culture of a whole tier of companies whose success is fundamental to the long-term health of their communities and the national economy.

For more information:

Nick Smith, President

or

Judy Burton, Administrator

700 Lonsdale Building
Duluth, MN 55802
218-722-0861
FAX 218-725-6800

SERIES A PREFERRED STOCK PURCHASE AGREEMENT

dated as of _____, 1996

by and among

NEWCO, Inc.

(the "Company"), and

Each of the Investors (the "Investors")
Listed in Exhibit 2.1

TABLE OF CONTENTS

ARTICLE IV

COVENANTS OF THE COMPANY

ARTICLE VII

MISCELLANEOUS

ARTICLE VIII

TERMINATION

ARTICLE IX

ARBITRATION

EXHIBITS

Community Development Venture Capital Transactions

Page

AGREEMENT dated _____, 199_, between Newco, Inc., a Delaware corporation and each of the Investors listed in Exhibit 2.1.

PREAMBLE

The Company wishes to obtain equity financing. The Investors are willing, on the terms contained in this Agreement, to purchase Series A Preferred Stock of the Company having the characteristics set forth in the Certificate of Designation, as amended, attached as Exhibit 1.1. Capitalized terms are defined in the first Article. Exhibits are incorporated by reference into this Agreement as though such exhibits were set forth at the point of such reference. The neuter gender shall include the masculine and feminine genders as appropriate.

ARTICLE I

DEFINED TERMS

The following terms, when used in this Agreement, have the following meanings, unless the context otherwise indicates:

"'33 Act" means the Securities Act of 1933.

"'34 Act" means the Securities Exchange Act of 1934.

"Affiliate" means, with respect to any specified Person, (1) any other Person who, directly or indirectly, owns or controls, is under common ownership or control with, or is owned or controlled by, such specified Person, (2) any other Person who is a director, officer or partner or is, directly or indirectly, the beneficial owner of ten (10) percent or more of any class of equity securities, of the specified Person or a Person described in clause (1) of this paragraph, (3) another Person of whom the specified Person is a director, officer or partner or is, directly or indirectly, the beneficial owner of ten (10) percent or more of any class of equity securities, (4) another Person in whom the specified Person has a substantial beneficial interest or as to whom the specified Person serves as trustee or in a similar capacity, or (5) any relative or spouse of the specified Person or any of the foregoing Persons, any relative of such spouse or any spouse of any such relative; provided, however, that at any time after the Closing Date, the Company and the Subsidiaries on the one hand and Seller and its Affiliates (other than the Company and the Subsidiaries) shall not be deemed to be Affiliates of each other.

"Best Knowledge" shall mean and include (a) actual knowledge of the Person, including, the actual knowledge of any of the officers or directors of the Company and the administrators of any of the facilities operated by the Company or any of its subsidiaries and (b) that knowledge which a prudent businessperson could have obtained in the management of his business after making due inquiry, and after exercising due diligence, with respect thereto.

"Bylaws" means the bylaws of Newco, Inc., as amended.

"Certificate of Incorporation" means the certificate of incorporation of Newco, Inc., as originally filed with the Delaware Secretary of State together with all amendments thereto.

"Certificate of Designation" means the certificate of designation adopted by the Newco board of directors establishing the rights, limitations, etc., of the Series A Preferred Stock.

"Closing" and "Closing Date" mean the consummation of the Company's sale and the Investors' purchase of the Series A Preferred Stock, and the date on which the same occurs or occurred.

"Commission" means the United States Securities and Exchange Commission.

"Common Stock" means the $.01 par value common stock of Newco, Inc.

"Employee Benefit Plan" means any plan regulated under the Employees Retirement and Income Supplement Act ("ERISA").

"Financial Statements" means any financial statements (including the Notes thereto) of Newco, Inc. certified by the Company's independent public accountants and any such statements not so certified but containing substantially all the information covered in such certified statements, including a balance sheet as of the end of a fiscal period and statements of income and retained earnings and of sources and applications of funds for such fiscal period, together with all notes thereto.

"Financial Statements" shall mean all of the following:

        (a)   the audited financial statements of the Company as of [the quarter prior to Closing] (including all schedules and notes thereto), consisting of the balance sheet at such date and the related statements of income and expenses, retained earnings, changes in financial position and cash flows for the twelve-month period then ended; and

(b)   the audited financial statements of the Company as of [close of quarter prior to Closing for which Company has audited financial statements] (including all schedules and notes thereto), consisting of the balance sheet at such date and the related statements of income and expenses, retained earnings, changes in financial position and cash flows for the twelve (12) month period then ended.

In addition to (a) and (b) above, after the date of this Agreement, the term "Financial Statements" shall include any and all interim financial statements thereafter issued.

"Financial Statement Date" means the date of the most recent Financial Statements of the Company.

"Founders" means the signatories to this Agreement under the heading of <u>Founders.</u>

"Holder" means an Investor (or its successors or assigns) who continues to hold either Common Stock or Series A Preferred Stock.

"Independent Public Accountants" means that firm of independent certified public accountants selected by the Company's Board of Directors [with the approval of the Investor Directors].

"Investor Directors" means that individual or individuals who sit on the Company's Board of Directors at the request or insistence (whether by written agreement or otherwise) of the Investors.

"Offering Memorandum" means Newco, Inc.'s private offering memorandum dated _____, 1996.

"Qualified Holder" means an Investor or a transferee of an Investor or another Qualified Holder (assuming all such transfers were made in accordance with this Agreement) who holds of record [10%] or more of the shares of the Company's Common Stock or enjoys rights to purchase or convert into [10%] or more of the same, provided that (i) a transferee of an Investor who, in the reasonable judgment of Company, is affiliated with an actual or potential competitor of the Company may be deemed by the Company not to be a Qualified Holder; (ii) any Investor notifying the Company that it is a Venture Capital Operating Company within the meaning of the Department of Labor's Final Plan Asset Regulation, 29 C.F.R. Part 2510 (Mar. 13, 1987) shall be a Qualified Holder; and (iii) the general and limited partners, officers or Affiliates of an Investor.

"Qualified Public Offering" means both (i) the date of the effectiveness of any registration statement relating to the underwritten distribution Company's Common Stock which is filed by the Company under the '33 Act with proposed maximum offering proceeds to the Company (calculated in accordance with Rule 457 under the '33 Act, as such rule may be amended from time to time) of $5,000,000 or more and the public offering price is not less than $10.00 per share (as adjusted from time to time upon the occurrence of any subdivision, stock split, combination or change of Common Stock into a different number of shares of the same or any other class or classes of shares), and (ii) the process of distributing such common stock to the public.

"Series A Preferred Stock" means the $.01 par value cumulative convertible preferred stock, Series A of Newco, Inc. having the characteristics set forth in the Certificate of Designation.

"Shares" means any shares of the Company's Series A Preferred Stock or Common Stock, as the context requires.

"Subscription Agreement" means the subscription agreement executed by each Investor, the terms of which are incorporated herein and made a part hereof.

"Subsidiary" or "Subsidiaries" of any Person means any corporation or other entity of which securities or other ownership interests having ordinary voting power to elect a majority of the board of directors or other Persons performing similar functions are at the time directly or indirectly owned or controlled by such Person or one or more Subsidiaries of such Person.

Additional defined Terms are found in the body of the following text:

The masculine form of words includes the feminine and the neuter and vice versa, and, unless the context otherwise requires, the singular form of words includes the plural and vice versa. The words "herein," "hereof," "hereunder," and other words of similar import when used in this Agreement refer to this Agreement as a whole, and not to any particular section or subsection.

ARTICLE II

PURCHASE AND SALE TERMS

Section 2.1.   <u>Purchase and Sale</u>.   Subject to the terms of this Agreement, the Company shall issue and sell to the Investors and each Investor shall purchase from the Company at the Closing the number of shares of Series

A Preferred Stock at the aggregate purchase price set forth opposite its name in Exhibit 2.1. The obligation of each Investor to purchase is several and not joint.

Section 2.2. Payment. Each of the Investors shall pay the purchase price of the Series A Preferred Stock purchased by it in full at the Closing in cash, certified check or other means of payment acceptable to the Company.

Section 2.3. Transfer Legends and Restrictions. The transfer of the Shares will be restricted in accordance with the terms hereof. Each certificate evidencing the Shares, including any certificate issued to any transferee thereof, shall be imprinted with legends in substantially the following form (unless otherwise permitted under this Section or unless such Shares shall have been effectively registered and sold under the '33 Act and the applicable state securities laws):

"THESE SHARES HAVE NOT BEEN REGISTERED UNDER THE '33 ACT. THEY MAY NOT BE OFFERED OR TRANSFERRED BY SALE, ASSIGNMENT, PLEDGE OR OTHERWISE UNLESS (I) A REGISTRATION STATEMENT FOR THE SHARES UNDER THE SECURITIES ACT IS IN EFFECT OR (II) THE COMPANY HAS RECEIVED AN OPINION OF COUNSEL, WHICH OPINION IS SATISFACTORY TO THE COMPANY, TO THE EFFECT THAT SUCH REGISTRATION IS NOT REQUIRED UNDER THE SECURITIES ACT. TRANSFER OF THESE SHARES IS FURTHER RESTRICTED AS PROVIDED IN THE SERIES A PREFERRED STOCK PURCHASE AGREEMENT DATED _____, 199_, A COPY OF WHICH IS AVAILABLE AT THE COMPANY'S OFFICES."

The Holder of any Shares by acceptance thereof agrees, so long as any legend described in this Section shall remain on the certificates evidencing the Shares, prior to any transfer of any of the same (except for a transfer effected pursuant to an effective registration statement under the '33 Act or in compliance with Rule 144 or Rule 144A thereunder), to give written notice to the Company of such Holder's intention to effect such transfer and agrees to comply in all material respects with the provisions of this Section. Such notice, if required, shall describe the proposed method of transfer of the Shares in question. Upon receipt by the Company of such notice, if required, and if in the opinion of counsel to such Holder, which opinion shall be reasonably satisfactory to the Company, the proposed transfer may be effected without registration under the '33 Act in compliance with Section 4(2) or Rules 144 or 144A thereunder and under applicable state securities laws, then the proposed transfer may be effected; provided, however, that in the case of any Holder which is a partnership, no such opinion of counsel shall be necessary for a transfer by such partnership to a partner of such partnership, or a retired partner of such partnership who retires after the date such partnership became a Holder, or the estate of any such partner or retired partner, if the transferee agrees in writing to be subject to the terms of this Section to the same extent as if such transferee were originally a signatory to this Agreement. Upon receipt by the Company of such opinion and of such agreement by the transferee to be bound by this Section, the Holder of such Shares shall thereupon be entitled to transfer the same in accordance with the terms of the notice (if any) delivered by such Holder to the Company. Each certificate evidencing the Shares issued upon any such transfer shall bear the legend set forth in this Section. Upon the written request of a Holder of the Shares, the Company shall remove the foregoing legend from the certificates evidencing such Shares and issue to such Holder new certificates therefor, free of any transfer legend if, with such request, the Company shall have received an opinion of counsel selected by the Holder, such opinion to be reasonably satisfactory to the Company, to the effect that any transfers by said Holder of such Shares may be made to the public without compliance with either Section 5 of the '33 Act or Rule 144 thereunder and with applicable state securities laws. In no event will such legend be removed if such opinion is based upon the "private offering" exemption of Section 4(2) of the '33 Act.

ARTICLE III

REPRESENTATIONS AND WARRANTIES OF THE COMPANY

Except as set forth in the Exhibits furnished pursuant to this Agreement, the Company [and certain Founders] represent[s] and warrant[s] [severally, or jointly and severally] to the Investors, at and as of the Closing that:

Section 3.1.   Corporate Existence. The Company is a corporation duly incorporated, validly existing and in good standing under Delaware law and has unconditional power and authority to conduct its business and own its properties as now conducted and owned. Exhibit 3.1 is a true copy of the Certificate of Incorporation, with all amendments. The Company is qualified as a foreign corporation to do business in all jurisdictions in which the nature of its properties and business requires such qualification [and in which noncompliance with such qualification would materially affect the Company's business].

Section 3.2.   Power and Authority. The Company has unconditional power and authority, and has taken all required corporate and other action necessary (including stockholder approval, if necessary) to permit it to own and hold properties to carry on its current business, to execute and deliver this Agreement, to issue and sell the Series A Preferred Stock as herein provided and otherwise to carry out the terms of this Agreement and all other documents, instruments, or transactions required by this Agreement, and none of such actions will violate any provision of the Company's Bylaws or Certificate of Incorporation, or result in the breach of or constitute a default under any agreement or instrument to which the Company is a party or by which it is bound or result in the creation or imposition of any material lien, claim or encumbrance on any Company asset. This Agreement has been duly executed and delivered by the Company and (assuming the due authorization, execution and delivery hereof by the Investors) constitutes the valid and binding obligation of the Company enforceable against the Company in accordance with its terms. No event has occurred and no condition exists which would constitute a violation of this Agreement. Neither this Agreement nor any other gives any person rights to terminate any agreements with the Company or otherwise to exercise rights against the Company.

Section 3.3. Financial Condition. The Company has previously furnished to the Investors its Financial Statements, which, together with the footnotes thereto, are complete and correct, have been prepared in accordance with generally accepted accounting principles ("GAAP") consistently applied, and fairly present the financial condition of the Company as of the dates specified.

Section 3.3.1. Absence of Undisclosed Liabilities. As of the Financial Statement Date, the Company had (and on the date hereof the Company has) no material liabilities (matured or unmatured, fixed or contingent, which are not fully reflected or provided for on the balance sheet of the Company as of the Financial Statement Date), or any material loss contingency (as defined in Statement of Financial Accounting Standards No. 5) whether or not required by GAAP to be shown on the Balance Sheets, except (i) obligations to perform under commitments incurred in the ordinary course of business after the Financial Statement Date, (ii) tax and related liabilities due and specifically set forth in Exhibit 3.3.1, which liabilities shall be fully paid concurrently with the Closing as provided in Exhibit 3.3.1, and (iii) other liabilities as set forth in Exhibit 3.3.1.

Section 3.3.2. Taxes. For all periods ended on or prior to the Financial Statement Date, the Company has accurately completed and filed or will file within the time prescribed by law (including extensions of time approved by the appropriate taxing authority) all tax returns and reports required to be filed with the Internal Revenue Service, the State of Delaware, any other states or governmental subdivisions and all foreign countries and has paid, or made adequate provision in the Financial Statements dated the Financial Statement Date for the payment of, all taxes, interest, penalties, assessments or deficiencies shown to be due (or, to the knowledge of the Company [or any

Founders], claimed by such authority or jurisdiction to be due) on or in respect of such tax returns and reports. The Company [and the Founders] know[s] of (a) no other federal, Delaware, state, county, municipal or foreign taxes which are due and payable by the Company which have not been so paid; (b) no other federal, Delaware, state, county, municipal or foreign tax returns or reports which are required to be filed which have not been so filed; and (c) no unpaid assessment for additional taxes for any fiscal period or any basis thereof; except for taxes which are due and are specifically set forth in Exhibit 3.3.2 hereto but which shall be paid in full concurrently with the Closing as provided in Exhibit 3.3.2. The Company's federal or state income tax returns have never been audited [have been audited through the Company's fiscal year ending in 19__]. Proper and accurate amounts have been withheld by the Company from its employees for all periods in compliance with the tax, social security and any employment withholding provisions of applicable federal and state law. Proper and accurate, in all material respects, federal and state returns have been filed by the Company for all periods for which returns were due with respect to employee income tax withholding, social security and unemployment taxes, and the amounts shown thereon to be due and payable have been paid in full or provision therefor included on the books of the Company in accordance with and to the extent required by GAAP. The Company has not made any election under Section 341(f) of the Internal Revenue Code of 1986, as amended (the "Code").

Section 3.3.3.   Subsidiaries. The Company has no subsidiaries and owns no capital stock or other securities, or rights or obligations to acquire the same, of any other entity.

or

Section 3.3.3.   Subsidiaries. Exhibit 3.3.3 hereto sets forth a list of all Subsidiaries of the Company. Each Subsidiary is a corporation duly organized, validly existing and in good standing under the laws of its jurisdiction of incorporation as stated on the said Exhibit 3.3.3, has all requisite corporate power and authority to own, lease and operate its properties and to carry on its business as now being conducted, and is duly qualified as a foreign corporation in all jurisdictions in which it is required to be so qualified. Each Subsidiary is wholly owned by the Company and no Person has any right to participate in, or receive any payment based on any amount relating to, the revenue, income, value or net worth of the Subsidiaries or any component or portion thereof, or any increase or decrease in any of the foregoing.

Section 3.4.   No Material Adverse Change. Since the Financial Statement Date there has been no material adverse change in the financial or other condition, properties or business operations of the Company.

Section 3.5.   <u>Litigation</u>.   There are no suits, proceedings or investigations pending or threatened against or affecting the Company or an officer of the Company which could have a material adverse effect on the business, assets, or financial condition of the Company or the ability of any officer to participate in the affairs of the Company, or which concern [in any material way] the transactions contemplated by the Agreement. The foregoing includes, without limiting its generality, actions pending or threatened (or any basis therefor known to the Company) involving the prior employment of any employees or currently contemplated prospective employees of the Company or their use, in connection with the business of the Company, of any information or techniques which might be alleged to be proprietary to their former employer(s).

Section 3.5.1.   <u>Conflict of Interests</u>.   Neither the Company nor any officer, employee, agent or any other person acting on behalf of the Company has, directly or indirectly, given or agreed to give any money, gift or similar benefit (other than legal price concessions to customers in the ordinary course of business) to any customer, supplier, employee or agent of a customer or supplier, or official or employee of any governmental agency or instrumentality of any government (domestic or foreign) or other Person who was, is, or may be in of a position to help or hinder the business of the Company (or assist in connection with any actual or proposed transaction) which (a) might subject the Company to any damage or penalty in any civil, criminal or governmental litigation or proceeding, (b) if not given in the past, might have had a material adverse effect on the assets, business or operations of the Company as reflected in the Financial Statements, or (c) if not continued in the future, might materially adversely affect the assets, business, operations or prospects of the Company.

Section 3.5.2.   <u>Other Relationships</u>.   Except as set forth in <u>Exhibit 3.5.2</u>, to the best knowledge of the Company, the officers of the Company have no interest (other than as noncontrolling holders of securities of a publicly traded company), either directly or indirectly, in any entity, including without limitation, any corporation, partnership, joint venture, proprietorship, firm, person, licensee, business or association (whether as an employee, officer, director, shareholder, agent, independent contractor, security holder, creditor, consultant, or otherwise) that presently (i) provides any services or designs, produces and/or sells any products or product lines, or engages in any activity which is the same, similar to or competitive with any activity or business in which the Company is now engaged; (ii) is a supplier of, customer of, creditor of, or has an existing contractual relationship with the Company; or (iii) has any direct or indirect interest in any asset or property used by the Company or any property, real or personal, tangible or intangible, that is necessary or desirable for the conduct of the business of the Company. Except as set forth in <u>Exhibit 3.5.2</u> hereto, no current or former stockholder, director, officer or employee of the Company nor any Affiliate of any such person, is at present, or since the inception of the Company has been, directly or indirectly through his or her affiliation with any other person or entity, a party to any transaction (other than as an employee) with the Company providing for the furnishing of services by, or rental of real or personal property from, or otherwise requiring cash payments to any such person.

Section 3.6.   Licenses; Compliance with Laws, Other Agreements, etc. The Company has all franchises, permits, licenses, and other rights which it currently deems necessary for the conduct of its business and it knows of no basis for the denial of such rights in the future. The Company is not in material violation of any order or decree of any court, or of the provisions of any contract or agreement to which it is a party or by which it may be bound, or, to its knowledge, of any law, order, or regulation of any governmental authority, and neither this Agreement nor the transactions contemplated hereby will result in any such violation.

Section 3.6.1.   Intellectual Property Rights and Government Approvals. Included in Exhibit 3.6.1 is a true and complete list and summary description of all patents, trademarks, service marks, trade names, copyrights (which have been filed with the federal copyright authorities) and rights or licenses to use the same, and any and all applications therefor, presently owned or held by the Company. To the Founders' knowledge (the Company making this representation and warranty without such qualification), such patents, trademarks, service marks, trade names, copyrights and rights or licenses to use the same, and any and all applications therefor, as well as all trade secrets and similar proprietary information owned or held by the Company, are all that are required to enable the Company to conduct its business as now conducted, and the Company believes that it either now owns, has the right to use, possesses or will be able to obtain possession of or develop, and (with respect to its trade secrets and similar proprietary information) has provided adequate safeguards and security for the protection of, all such rights which it will require to conduct its business as proposed to be conducted as described in the Offering Memorandum. Neither the Company nor any of the Founders has received any formal or informal notice of infringement or other complaint that the Company's operations traverse or infringe rights under patents, trademarks, service marks, trade names, trade secrets, copyrights or licenses or any other proprietary rights of others, nor do the Company or the Founders have any reason to believe that there has been any such infringement. No person affiliated with the Company has wrongfully employed any trade secrets or any confidential information or documentation proprietary to any former employer, and no person affiliated with the Company has violated any confidential relationship which such person may have had with any third party. The Company has and will have full right and authority to utilize the processes, systems and techniques presently employed by it in the design, development and manufacture of its present products and all of its other products contemplated by the Offering Memorandum and all rights to any processes, systems and techniques developed by any employee or consultant of the Company have been and will be duly and validly assigned to the Company. No royalties, honorariums or fees are or will be payable by the Company to other persons by reason of the ownership or use by the Company of said patents, trademarks, service marks, trade names, trade secrets, copyrights or rights or licenses to use the same or similar proprietary information, or any and all applications therefor. The Company has all material governmental approvals, authorizations, consents, licenses and permits necessary or required to conduct its business as described in the Offering Memorandum. Each Founder for him or herself (and the Company to its knowledge with respect to all Founders) represents and warrants that no Founder, no associate of any Founder nor any other employee of the Company owns nor holds, directly or indirectly, any interests in any patents, trademarks, service marks, trade names, trade secrets, copyrights, licenses, inventions, any and all applications therefor, or any other proprietary rights used or currently contemplated to be used by the Company.

Section 3.6.2. Government Approvals. Except as may be required by any state "blue sky" laws, no authorization, consent, approval, license, qualification or formal exemption from, nor any filing, declaration or registration with, any court, governmental agency, regulatory authority or political subdivision thereof, any securities exchange or any other Person is required in connection with the execution, delivery or performance by the Company of this Agreement or the business of the Company or any of its Subsidiaries in order to consummate the transactions contemplated in this Agreement. All such material authorizations, consents, approvals, licenses, qualifications, exemptions, filings, declarations and registrations have been obtained or made, as the case may be, and are in full force and effect and are not the subject of any pending or, to the knowledge of the Company, threatened attack by appeal or direct proceeding or otherwise.

Section 3.6.3. Investment Company Act. The Company is not, and immediately after the Closing will not be, an "investment company" or a company "controlled" by an "investment company" within the meaning of the Investment Company Act.

Section 3.7. Ownership and Status of Stock. Exhibit 3.7 sets forth the number and par value of the shares of stock that the Company is currently authorized to issue, has issued, has outstanding and has reserved for issuance upon conversion of shares of Series A Preferred Stock into Common Stock. All the outstanding Common Stock is, and upon issuance and payment therefor in accordance with the terms of this Agreement, all of the outstanding shares of the

Series A Preferred Stock will be, validly issued, fully paid and nonassessable. All the outstanding Common Stock has been issued in full compliance with applicable law. None of the shares of the Common Stock or the Series A Preferred Stock are held in the Company's treasury. The Common Stock and the Series A Preferred Stock are not entitled to cumulative voting rights, preemptive rights, antidilution rights and so-called registration rights under the '33 Act, except as otherwise provided in this Agreement or in the powers, designations, rights and preferences of the Series A Preferred Stock contained in the Certificate of Designation. The Common Stock and the Series A Preferred Stock have the preferences, voting powers, qualifications, and special or relative rights or privileges set forth in the Certificate of Incorporation. The Company has outstanding no option, warrant or other commitment to issue or to acquire any shares of its capital stock, or any securities or obligations convertible into or exchangeable for its capital stock, except for the conversion provisions of the Series A Preferred Stock, nor, except as contemplated hereby, has it given any person any right to acquire from the Company or sell to the Company any shares of its capital stock. There is, and immediately upon consummation of the transactions contemplated hereby there will be, no agreement, restriction or encumbrance with respect to the sale or voting of any shares of capital stock of the Company (whether outstanding or issuable upon conversion or exercise of outstanding securities) except for the offering and sale of Series A Preferred Stock pursuant to this Agreement. Except as set forth in this Agreement, the Company has no obligation to register any of its presently outstanding securities or any of its securities which may thereafter be issued under the Act of 1933, as amended (the "'33 Act").

Section 3.8.   Private Sale.   The Company has not, either directly or through any agent, offered any securities to or solicited any offers to acquire any securities from, or otherwise approached, negotiated, or communicated in respect of any securities with, any person in such a manner as to require that the offer or sale of such securities (including but not limited to the Series A Preferred Stock) be registered pursuant to the provisions of Section 5 of the '33 Act and the rules and regulations of the Commission thereunder or the securities laws of any state and neither the Company nor anyone acting on its behalf will take any action prior to the Closing that would cause any such registration to be required (including, without limitation, any offer, issuance or sale of any security of the Company under circumstances which might require the integration of such security with the Series A Preferred Stock under the '33 Act or the rules and regulations of the Securities and Exchange Commission (the "Commission") thereunder) which might subject the offering, issuance or sale of the Series A Preferred Stock to the registration provisions of the '33 Act. The issuance of Series A Preferred Stock and the issuance of shares of Common Stock issuable upon the conversion of the Series A Preferred Stock, are exempt from registration under the '33 Act. The Company has complied with all federal and state securities and blue sky laws in all issuances and purchases of its capital stock prior to the date hereof and has not violated any applicable law in making such issuances and purchases of its capital stock prior to the date hereof. Any notices required to be filed under federal and state securities and blue sky laws prior to or subsequent to the Closing shall be filed on a timely basis prior to or as so required. Neither the Company nor any person authorized or employed by the Company as agent, broker, dealer or otherwise in connection with the offering or sale of the Series A Preferred Stock of the Company has offered the same or any such securities for sale to, or solicited any offers to buy the same from, or otherwise approached or negotiated with respect thereto with, any person or persons other than the Investors and not more than [ ] other financially sophisticated investors.

Section 3.9. Offering Memorandum. The Company has furnished the Investors with a copy of the Offering Memorandum which was prepared with reasonable care and sets forth a complete and accurate description of all plans, agreements and arrangements by which the Company may be bound and certain financial and other information concerning the Company. The Company and the Founders do not represent or warrant that any occurrences, developments or facts including, without limitation, projections, which the Offering Memorandum says will occur or eventuate after its date (or which were otherwise furnished in writing to the Investors), will in fact occur or eventuate after such date, but the Company and the Founders represent and warrant that such occurrences, developments or facts, including such projections, presented therein were prepared by the Company in good faith based on its best knowledge, information and belief. The Offering Memorandum read in connection with materials made available to the Investors by the Company (whether prepared by the Company or a third party) does not contain any untrue statement of a material fact nor does it omit to state any material fact necessary to make the statement therein not misleading. The information contained in the Offering Memorandum has been material to the Investors in their decision to invest.

Section 3.10. Investigation. It shall be no defense to an action for breach of this Agreement that the Investors or their agents have (or have not) made investigations into the affairs of the Company or that the Company [or the Founders] could not have known of the misrepresentation or breach of warranty. Damages for breach of a representation or warranty or other provision of this Agreement shall not be diminished by alleged tax savings resulting to the complaining party as a result of the loss complained of.

Section 3.10.1. Minute Books. The minute books of the Company contain a complete summary of all meetings of directors and stockholders since the time of incorporation and reflect all transactions referred to in such minutes accurately in all material respects.

Section 3.11.   Section 83(b) Elections.   To the best of the Company's knowledge, all elections and notices required by Section 83(b) of the Internal Revenue Code and any analogous provisions of applicable state tax laws have been timely filed by all individuals who have purchased shares of the Company's Common Stock and the Company has been notified of the same and will be so notified in the future.

Section 3.12.   Employment   Contracts,   etc.;   Certain   Material Transactions. Except as set forth in Exhibit 3.12 hereto, (i) the Company is not a party to any employment or deferred compensation agreements, (ii) the Company does not have any bonus, incentive or profit-sharing plans, (iii) the Company does not have any pension, retirement or similar plans or obligations, whether funded or unfunded, of a legally binding nature or in the nature of informal understandings and (iv) there are no existing material arrangements or proposed material transactions between the Company and any officer or director or holder of more than ten percent (10%) of the capital stock of the Company. To the knowledge of the Company, **[name key employees]** have no plans to terminate their respective relationships with the Company and/or any of its Subsidiaries. Exhibit 3.12 hereto sets forth the name (and, where applicable, the title) of each person employed by the Company as of _____, 1996, whose total compensation (inclusive of salary and bonuses) for the fiscal year then ended exceeded [$_____] *{a CDVC may want to use this dollar figure as a way of monitoring the compensation of the management team and the founder, to ensure that its investment is not solely benefiting those few individuals}* as well as the specific amount paid during or accrued in respect of such fiscal year to or for the account of each such person (i) as basic salary and (ii) as bonus and other compensation.

Section 3.13.   Contracts and Commitments, etc.Except as set forth in Exhibit 3.13, the Company is not a party to any written or oral contract or commitment not made in the ordinary course of business and, whether or not made in the ordinary course of business, the Company is not a party to any written or oral [(i) contract or commitment with any labor union,] (ii) contract or commitment for the future purchase of fixed assets, materials, supplies, or equipment involving an amount in excess of [$____], (iii) contract of commitment for the employment of any officer, individual employee or other person on a full-time basis or any contract with any individual on a consulting basis, (iv) bonus, pension, profit-sharing, retirement, stock purchase, stock option, or extraordinary hospitalization, medical insurance or similar plan, contract or understanding in effect with respect to employees or any of them or the employees of others, (v) agreements, indentures or commitments relating to the borrowing of money or to the mortgaging, pledging or otherwise placing of a lien on any assets of the Company, (vi) guaranty of any obligation for borrowed money or otherwise, (vii) lease or agreement under which the Company is lessor of or permits any third party to hold or operate any property, real or personal, owned or controlled by the Company, (viii) agreement or other commitment for capital expenditures in excess of [$_____] in the aggregate, (ix) contract or agreement under which the Company is obligated to pay any broker's fees, finder's fees or any such similar fees to any third party, (x) contract, agreement or commitment under which the Company has issued, or may become obligated to issue, any shares of capital stock of the Company, or any warrants, options, convertible securities or other commitments pursuant to which the Company is or may become obligated to issue any shares of its Common Stock, or (xi) any other contract, agreement, arrangement or understanding which is material to the business of the Company or which is material to a prudent investor's understanding of the business of the Company. The Company has furnished to counsel for the Investors true and correct copies of such agreements and other documents requested by the Investors or their authorized representatives.

Section 3.14.   Employee Benefit Plans.

Section 3.14.1.   Employee Benefit Plans and Employment Agreements. Except as listed on Exhibit 3.14.1 hereto, the Company is not a party to nor participates or has participated in (a) any profit-sharing, deferred compensation, bonus, stock option, stock purchase, pension, retainer, consulting, retirement, welfare or incentive plan or agreement whether legally binding or not, (b) any plan providing for "fringe benefits" to its employees, including but not limited to vacation, sick leave, medical, hospitalization, life insurance and other insurance plans, and related benefits, (c) any employment agreement not terminable on thirty (30) days (or less) written notice, or (d) any other "employee benefit plan" (within the meaning of Section 3(3) of the Employee Retirement Income Security Act of 1974 ("ERISA")). True, correct and complete copies of all documents with respect to the plans and agreements referred to in Exhibit 3.14.1 and all related summary plan descriptions have been delivered to counsel to the Investors. There are no negotiations, demands or proposals which are pending or have been made which concern matters now covered, or that would be covered, by the type of agreements or plans listed in this Section. The Company is in full compliance with the applicable provisions of ERISA (as amended by the Omnibus Budget Reconciliation Act of 1987, the Tax Reform Act of 1986, Retirement Equity Act of 1984, the Deficit Reduction Act of 1984, and the Tax Equity and Fiscal Responsibility Act of 1982) and the regulations and published authorities thereunder with respect to all such employee benefit plans. The Company is in full compliance with all other statutes, orders or governmental rules and regulations applicable to such plans.

The Company has performed all of its obligations under all such plans. There are no actions, suits or claims (other than routine claims for benefits) pending or threatened against such plans or the assets of such plans, and to the best knowledge of the Company, no facts exist which could give rise to any actions, suits or claims (other than routine claims for benefits) against such plans or the assets of such plans.

Section 3.14.2.   <u>Pension and Profit-Sharing Plans</u>.   The Employee Benefit Plans described on <u>Exhibit 3.14.2</u> have been duly authorized by the Board of Directors of Company. Each such plan is qualified in form and operation under Sections 401(a) and 501(a) of the Internal Revenue Code of 1986 (the "Code") and no event has occurred which will or could give rise to disqualification of any such plan under said Sections. No event has occurred which will or could subject any such plans to tax under Section 511 of the Code. No prohibited transaction (within the meaning of Section 4975 of the Code) or party-in-interest transaction (within the meaning of Section 406 of ERISA) has occurred with respect to any of such Plans. All costs of Plans have been provided for on the basis of consistent methods in accordance with sound actuarial assumptions and practices. As of the last valuation date for each of the Plans listed which are pension plans ("Employee Benefit Pension Plans") within the meaning of Section 3(2) of ERISA, the assets of such plan exceeded (or were less than the benefit liability of such plan), computed on a plan termination basis, by at least the amount shown below (or, in the case of an underfunded plan, by no more than the amount shown below):

Plan	Amounts by which assets exceed (or are less <u>than)</u> <u>benefit liability on a plan termination basis</u>
	$_____
	$_____
	$_____
	$_____

Since the last valuation date for each Employee Pension Benefit Plan, there has been no amendment or change thereunder and, to the knowledge of Company, there has been no event or occurrence which would cause the excess of assets over benefit liabilities listed above to be reduced or the amount by which liabilities exceeded assets as listed above to be increased. Company has delivered to counsel for the Investors for each of the Employee Pension Benefit

Plans (a) a copy of the Form 5500 which was filed in each of the most recent three plan years, including, without limitation, all schedules thereto and all financial statements with attached opinions of independent accountants, (b) a copy of the Form PBGC-1 which was filed in each of the most recent three Plan years, and (c) the most recent determination letter from the Internal Revenue Service. Copies have been furnished to such counsel of (a) the consolidated statement of assets and liabilities of each of the Employee Pension Benefit Plans as of its most recent valuation date; (b) the statement of changes in fund balance and in financial position or the statement of changes in net assets available for benefits under each of said Plans for the most recently ended plan year, and, (c) with respect to any such Plan which is subject to Title IV of ERISA, the actuarial report as of the last valuation date. Such documents fairly present the financial condition of each of said Plans as at such dates and the results of operations of each of said Plans, all in accordance with generally accepted accounting principles applied on a consistent basis.

Section 3.14.3. <u>Title IV Plans</u>. With respect to each Employee Pension Benefit Plan (excluding plans not subject to the provisions of Title IV of ERISA) listed on <u>Exhibit 3.14.3</u> or in which the Company (for purposes of this subsection 3.14.3 the "Company" shall include all trades or businesses whether or not incorporated, which are a member of a group of which Company is a member and which are under common control within the meaning of Section 414 of the Code and the regulations thereunder) participates or has participated, (a) the Company has not withdrawn from such a Plan during a plan year in which it was "substantial employer" (as defined in Section 4001(a)(2) of ERISA), (b) the Company has not filed a notice of intent to terminate any such Plan nor adopted any amendment to treat such Plan as terminated, (c) the Pension Benefit Guarantee Corporation ("PBGC") has not instituted proceedings to terminate any such Plan, (d) no other event or condition has occurred which might constitute grounds under Section 4042 of ERISA for the termination of, or the appointment of a trustee to administer, any such Plan, (e) no accumulated funding deficiency, whether or not waived, exists with respect to any such Plan, no condition has occurred or exists which by the passage of time would be expected to result in an accumulated funding deficiency as of the last day of the current Plan year of any such Plan, and the Company has not failed to make full payment when due of all amounts which under the provisions of any such Plan are required to be made as contributions thereto, (f) all required premium payments to the PBGC have been paid when due, (g) no reportable event, as described in Section 4043 of ERISA and the regulations thereunder, has occurred with respect to said plans, and (h) no excise taxes are payable under the Code.

Section 3.14.4. <u>Multiemployer Plans</u>. With respect to each Employee Pension Benefit Plan which is a "multiemployer plan" (within the meaning of Section 3(37) of ERISA) listed on Exhibit 3.14.4 or in which the Company participates or has participated, (a) the Company has not withdrawn, partially withdrawn, or received any notice of any claim or demand for withdrawal liability or partial withdrawal liability against any of them, (b) the Company has not received any notice that any such Plan is in reorganization, that increased contributions may be required to avoid a reduction in plan benefits or the imposition of any excise tax, or that any such Plan is or may become insolvent, (c) the Company has not failed to make any required contributions to any such Plan, (d) no such Plan is a party to any pending merger of asset or liability transfer, (e) there are no Pension Benefit Guaranty Corporation proceedings against any such plan, and (f) the Company has not (or will have as a result of the transactions contemplated hereby) any contingent liability for withdrawal liability by reason of a sale of assets pursuant to Section 4204 of ERISA.

Section 3.14.5.   Continuation Coverage Requirements of Health Plans. All group health plans of the Company (including any plans of affiliates of the Company which must be taken into account under Section 162(i) or (k) of the Code) have been operated in compliance with the group health plan continuation coverage requirements of Section 162(k) of the code to the extent such requirements are applicable.

Section 3.14.6.   Fines and Penalties. There have been no acts or omissions by the Company which have given rise to or may give rise to fines, penalties, taxes, or related charges under §§ 502(c) or (k) or 4071 of ERISA or Chapter 43 of the Code.

Section 3.15.   Banks, Agents, etc.   Exhibit 3.15 hereto contains a complete and correct list setting forth the name of (i) each bank in which the Company has an account, safe deposit box or borrowing privilege and the names of all persons authorized to draw thereon, to have access thereto or to borrow thereupon, as the case may be, and (ii) each agent to whom such corporation has granted a written power of attorney or similar authority to act on its behalf.

Section 3.16.   Small Business Concern. The Company is a "small business concern" as defined in § 121.3-11 of Title 13 of the Code of Federal Regulations. The Company has heretofore furnished to each Investor that is an SBIC the following completed forms: Size Status Declaration on SBA Form 480, Assurance of Compliance on SBA Form 652D, and Portfolio Financing Report on SBA Form 1031. The Company represents and warrants the completeness and correctness of each of said forms.

Section 3.17. <u>Environmental Liabilities</u>. The Company has not caused or allowed, nor has it contracted with any party for, the generation, use, transportation, treatment, storage or disposal of any Hazardous Substance (as defined below) in connection with the operations of its business or otherwise. The Company, together with any real property that it owns, leases, or otherwise occupies or uses and the operations of its business (the "Premises") are in compliance with all applicable Environmental Laws (as defined below) and orders or directives or any governmental authorities having jurisdiction under such Environmental Laws, including, without limitation, any Environmental Laws or orders or directives with respect to any cleanup or remediation of any release or threat of release of Hazardous Substances. The Company has not received any citation, directive, letter or other communication, written or oral, or any notice of any proceedings, claims or lawsuits, from any person, entity or governmental authority arising out of the ownership or occupation of the Premises or the conduct of its operations, nor is it aware of any basis therefor. The Company has obtained and is maintaining in full force and effect all necessary permits, licenses and approvals required by any Environmental Laws applicable to the Premises and the business operations conducted thereon (including operations conducted by tenants on the Premises), and is in compliance with all such permits, licenses and approvals. The Company has not caused or allowed a release, or a threat of release, of any Hazardous Substance unto, at or near the Premises nor, to its best knowledge, has the Premises or any property at or near the Premises ever been subject to a release, or a threat of release, of any Hazardous Substance. For purposes of this Agreement, the term "Environmental Laws" shall mean any federal, state or local law, ordinance or regulation pertaining to the protection of human health or the environment, including without limitation, the Comprehensive Environmental Response, Compensation and Liability Act, 42 U.S.C. §§ 9601 <u>et</u> <u>seq</u>., Emergency Planning and Community Right-to-Know Act, 42 U.S.C. §§ 11001 <u>et</u> <u>seq</u>., and the Resource Conservation and Recovery Act, 42 U.S.C. §§ 6901 <u>et</u> <u>seq</u>. For purposes of this Agreement, the term "Hazardous Substances" shall include oil and petroleum products, asbestos, polychlorinated biphenyls and urea formaldehyde, and any other materials classified as hazardous or toxic under any Environmental Laws.

ARTICLE IV

COVENANTS OF THE COMPANY

Section 4.1. <u>Accounts and Reports</u>. Until a Qualified Public Offering occurs, the Company shall furnish to each Qualified Holder copies of the following certificates, filings and reports:

(a)   Annual Reports. As soon as available, and in any event within ninety (90) days after the end of each fiscal year, Financial Statements of the Company.

(b)   Quarterly Reports. As soon as available, and in any event within forty-five (45) days after the end of each of the first three quarters of each fiscal year, unaudited Financial Statements of the Company. All such statements shall set forth in comparative form the figures for the corresponding periods of the preceding fiscal year, and shall be prepared in reasonable detail and in accordance with generally accepted accounting principles consistently applied. [Each of such quarterly financial statements shall be accompanied by a report of the president of the Company explaining business developments and problems occurring during the relevant quarter and a discussion of the figures presented in such financial statements.]

(c)   Monthly Financial Statements. Within fifteen (15) days after the end of each month, copies of the Company's comparative statements of income and cash flow and unaudited, consolidated balance sheet as of the end of such month, which shall be prepared in accordance with generally accepted accounting principles consistently applied [and so certified by the Company's principal financial officer].

Comment: *Some CDVCs require reporting on progress toward social goals of business - for example, employment figures. These can be required on a monthly, quarterly or annual basis, as is appropriate.*

(d)   Certifications. All financial statements referred to in section (a) above, if not certified by the Company's Independent Public Accountants, shall be certified as accurate and complete in all material respects (subject to normal year-end adjustments) by the chief executive and chief financial officers of the Company and shall be presented in form comparative to the similar period of the preceding year. If for any period the Company has any subsidiary or subsidiaries whose accounts are consolidated with those of the Company, then in respect of such period all such financial statements will be the consolidated and consolidating financial statements of the Company and all such consolidated subsidiaries.
All such financial statements may be labelled "confidential" by the Company. In any event, without the Company's express consent, the recipient will make no use or disclosure of the financial statements except in connection with evaluating its investment in the Company.

(e)   <u>Forecasts</u>. As soon as available, but in no event later than one month after the start of each fiscal year, monthly financial forecasts and, promptly after preparation, any revisions thereto, in a format approved by the Investor Directors, for the current fiscal year, [unless, in the opinion of counsel to the Company, providing any such forecast will require inclusion of the same in a subsequent Public Offering].

(f)   <u>Other Information</u>. Upon the reasonable request of a Qualified Holder, the Company will deliver to such Qualified Holder other information and data, not proprietary in nature (in the good-faith judgment of the Company), pertaining to its business, financial and corporate affairs to the extent that such delivery will not violate any then applicable laws and any contracts of the Company with third persons. The Company will permit any person designated by a Qualified Holder in writing, at the expense of such Qualified Holder, to visit and inspect any of the properties of the Company, including its books of account, and to discuss its affairs, finances, and accounts with the Company's officers or directors, all at such reasonable times and as often as a Qualified Holder may reasonably request, all in a manner consistent with the reasonable security and confidentiality needs of the Company, provided that the Company shall be under no such obligation (i) with respect to information deemed in good faith by the Company to be proprietary or (ii) if the Company's board of directors reasonably believes such visit, inspection, or discussion would violate applicable laws or any contract with third persons.

(g)   All information furnished under this Section is confidential and each recipient shall (i) maintain the same in confidence and (ii) take all reasonable measures to prevent any officer or agent of such recipient from disclosing the same. The preceding sentence notwithstanding, the Investors may, for the purpose of assessing and publicizing the progress of this and investments in other portfolio companies, use the information obtained pursuant to this Section in reports to third parties, provided the Investors will not, without the written permission of the Company, identify the Company by name or by any other information that might otherwise reveal the identity of the Company.

(h)   As soon as available, but not later than ninety (90) days after the end of each fiscal year of the Company, a certificate of the Company's certified public accountants certifying to the Investors that, based upon their examination of the affairs of the Company performed in connection with the preparation of such financial statements in accordance with generally accepted auditing standards, they are not aware of the occurrence or existence during such fiscal year of any condition or event which constitutes or would, upon notice or lapse of time or both, constitute a default in any of the Company's obligations under this Agreement or any other agreement to which the Company is a party, or, if they are aware of such condition or event, specifying to the Investors the nature thereof;

Section 4.2.   Use of Proceeds. The Company shall use the proceeds of the sale of the Series A Preferred Stock for working capital, and otherwise as set forth in the Offering Memorandum.

Section 4.3.   Exhibits. The Company will furnish all Exhibits and other attachments or enclosures to this Agreement at least two business days prior to the scheduled Closing Date.

Section 4.4.   Financial Covenants.

Rider 4.4

Section 4.5.   Social Covenants.

> Comment: *Affirmative social covenants can be inserted here regarding employment targets, environmental benefits, etc. (See Appendix A) Alternatively, it may make sense to attach as* Exhibit 4.5 *a "Social Covenant Agreement" or some other document memorializing the agreed upon social goals of the business. The text of this section could then commit the Company to the furtherance of those goals enumerated in the Exhibit. A negative covenant could be drafted and inserted below that provides for specific remedies in the event the Company materially breaches the Social Covenant Agreement (for example, the Investors could be entitled to "put" their stock, or control of the Board could shift to the Investors until such time as the breach is cured). Any such remedies would need to be carefully drafted with an eye towards (a) enforceability and effectiveness, (b) self-activation (in other words, the remedy, once triggered, should ideally not require a judicial proceeding to take effect), and (c) possible claims by minority shareholders of oppression by the Investors, or of breach of fiduciary duty.*

Section 4.6.   Compensation of Executive Officers. The salary and other compensation, including without limitation bonuses and fringe benefits, of the officers of the Company shall be as approved from time to time by the Board of Directors of the Company, including the Investor Directors.

Section 4.7.   Rule 144. The Investors recognize that the provisions of Rule 144 under the '33 Act are not presently applicable to securities of the

Company. The Company covenants that (a) at all times after the Company first becomes subject to the reporting requirements of Section 13 or 15(d) of the Exchange Act, the Company will comply with the current public information requirements of Rule 144(c)(1) under the '33 Act; and (b) at all such times as Rule 144 is available for use by the Investors, the Company will furnish any Investor upon request with all information within the possession of the Company required for the preparation and filing of Form 144.

Section 4.8. <u>Future Noncompetition and Proprietary Rights Agreements</u>.

(a) <u>Proprietary Information</u>. The Company shall use its best efforts to (i) insure that no person employed by the Company will wrongfully employ any confidential information or documentation proprietary to any former employer, (ii) protect, by maintenance of secrecy to the extent appropriate, all technical and business information developed by and belonging to the Company which has not been patented, (iii) cause to be patented all technological information developed by and belonging to the Company, which, in the opinion of the Company and its counsel, is patentable and is best protected by patenting, and (iv) cause each person who becomes an employee of the Company and who shall have access to confidential or proprietary information of the Company, to execute an agreement relating to matters of noncompetition and nondisclosure and assignment.

(b) <u>Licenses and Trademarks</u>. The Company shall use its best efforts to own, possess and maintain all patents, trademarks, service marks, trade names, copyrights and licenses necessary or useful in the conduct of its business, including, without limitation, such of the same as are listed in <u>Exhibit 3.6.1</u> hereto.

Section 4.9. <u>Stock Restriction Agreements For Future Employees</u>. The Company and each future employee or consultant purchasing or otherwise receiving shares of Common Stock from the Company (other than persons receiving Common Stock upon declaration of dividends or by conversion of preferred stock) will enter into a stock restriction agreement (or, upon grant of a stock option, an option agreement) in the form approved by the Board of Directors of the Company and the Investor Directors.

Section 4.10. <u>Observer Rights</u>. The Company will permit each Qualified Holder or any authorized representative thereof, to attend all meetings of the Board of Directors of the Company, and shall, upon the written request of such Qualified Holder, provide him, her or it with such notice of and other information with respect to such meetings as are delivered to the directors of the

Company. Upon the written request of any such Qualified Holder, the Company shall notify such holder, within ten (10) days thereafter of the taking of any written action by the Board of Directors of the Company in lieu of a meeting thereof. Any Qualified Holder exercising his or its rights under this subsection, and his or its representatives, shall maintain the confidentiality of all financial, confidential and proprietary information of the Company acquired by them in exercising such rights.

Section 4.11. Key-Person Insurance. The Company shall purchase and maintain life and disability insurance policies on the persons and in the benefit amounts set forth on Exhibit 4.11 hereto. The Company shall be the beneficiary of all such policies and the proceeds payable to the Company shall be used by the Company to refinance the redemption of shares of Series A Preferred Stock required by the Certificate of Designation or, if such redemption is either (i) unnecessary because of the prior conversion or redemption of such shares or (ii) illegal, to be used by the Company solely for product development purposes.

Section 4.12. Liability Insurance. The Company will maintain in full force and effect a policy or policies of standard comprehensive general liability insurance underwritten by a U.S. insurance company insuring its properties and business against such losses and risks, and in such amounts as are adequate for its business and as are customarily carried by entities of similar size engaged in the same or similar business. Such policies shall include property loss insurance policies, with extended coverage, sufficient in amount to allow the replacement of any of its tangible properties which might be damaged or destroyed by the risks or perils normally covered by such policies.

Section 4.13. Taxes and Assessments. The Company will pay and will cause each of its Subsidiaries to pay any taxes, assessments and governmental charges, and any liabilities thereon, outstanding as of the Closing Date. The Company will pay and discharge and will cause each of its Subsidiaries to pay and discharge, before the same become delinquent and before penalties accrue thereon, all taxes, assessments and governmental charges upon or against the Company or any of its Subsidiaries, or any of their respective properties, and all other material liabilities at any time existing, except to the extent and so long as (a) the same are being contested in good faith and by appropriate proceedings in such manner as not to cause any material adverse effect upon the financial condition of the Company or any of its Subsidiaries, or the loss of any right of redemption from any sale thereunder and (b) the Company or any of its Subsidiaries shall have set aside on its books adequate reserves with respect thereto.

Comment: *In the event that one or more of the Investors is a tax-exempt entity, it may be advisable to insert language here, or in a separate affirmative covenant, or in a negative covenant, to the effect that the Company will endeavor to avoid engaging in activities that might jeopardize the tax-exempt status of such Investor(s), perhaps with reference to Section 501(c)(3) of the Internal Revenue Code and to relevant I.R.S. memoranda and private letter rulings.*

Section 4.14.   Maintenance of Corporate Existence.   Unless otherwise determined by the Board of Directors of the Company, each of the Company and its Subsidiaries will preserve, renew and keep in full force and effect, its corporate existence, qualification in requisite jurisdictions and rights and privileges necessary or desirable in the normal conduct of its business.

Section 4.15.   Governmental Consents.   The Company will obtain all consents, approvals, licenses and permits required by federal, state, local and foreign law to carry on its business.

Section 4.16.   Further Assurances.   The Company will cure promptly any defects in the creation and issuance of the Shares, and in the execution and delivery of this Agreement.   The Company, at its expense, will promptly execute and deliver promptly to each Investor upon request all such other and further documents, agreements and instruments in compliance with or pursuant to its covenants and agreements herein, and will make any recordings, file any notices, and obtain any consents as may be necessary or appropriate in connection therewith.

Section 4.17.   Counsel Fees and Expenses.   The Company agrees to reimburse the reasonable fees and expenses of a single special counsel for the Investors up to a maximum amount of $_____.

Section 4.18.   Compliance with Offering Memorandum.   The Company agrees at all times to conduct its business in accordance with the Offering Memorandum, including the Use of Proceeds provisions, and to present to the Board of Directors for their prior approval (including the Investor Members) any proposed change in its operations which materially differs from said Offering Memorandum.

Section 4.19.   Regulation D Filings.   The Company will file on a timely basis all notices of sale required to be filed with the Securities and Exchange Commission (the "Commission") pursuant to Regulation D under the '33 Act with respect to the transactions contemplated by this Agreement and simultaneously furnish copies of each report of sale to each Investor.

Section 4.20.   Preemptive Rights.

(a)   The Company hereby grants to each Qualified Holder a right of first refusal to purchase, on a pro rata basis, all or any part of New Securities (as defined below) which the Company may, from time to time, propose the sell and issue subject to the terms and conditions set forth below. A Qualified Holder's pro rata share, for purposes of this subsection 4.20, shall equal a fraction, the numerator of which is the number of shares of Common Stock then held by such Qualified Holder or issuable upon conversion or exercise of any Shares, convertible securities, options, rights, or warrants then held by such Qualified Holder, and the denominator of which is the total number of shares of Common Stock then outstanding plus the number of shares of Common Stock issuable upon conversion or exercise of then outstanding Shares, convertible securities, options, rights or warrants.

(b)   "New Securities" shall mean any capital stock of the Company whether now authorized or not and rights, options or warrants to purchase capital stock, and securities of any type whatsoever which are, or may become, convertible into capital stock; provided, however, that the term "New Securities" does not include (i) the Shares issuable under this Agreement or the Shares of Common Stock issuable upon conversion of the Series A Preferred Stock; (ii) securities offered to the public pursuant to a Public Offering; (iii) securities issued for the acquisition of another corporation by the Company by merger, purchase of substantially all the assets of such corporation or other reorganization resulting in the ownership by the Company of not less than fifty-one percent (51%) of the voting power of such corporation; (iv) not more than _____ shares of Common Stock issued to employees or consultants of the Company pursuant to a stock option plan, employee stock purchase plan, restricted stock plan or other employee stock plan or agreement; or (v) securities issued as a result of any stock split, stock dividend or reclassification of Common Stock, distributable on a pro rata basis to all holders of Common Stock.

(c)   If the Company intends to issue New Securities, it shall give each Qualified Holder written notice of such intention, describing the type of New Securities to be issued, the price thereof and the general terms upon which the Company proposes to effect such issuance. Each Qualified Holder shall have twenty (20) days from the date of any such notice to agree to purchase all or part of its or his pro rata share of such New Securities for the price and upon the general terms and conditions specified in the Company's notice by giving written notice to the Company stating the quantity of New Securities to be so purchased. Each Qualified Holder shall have a right of overallotment such that if any Qualified Holder fails to exercise his or its right hereunder to purchase his or its total pro rata portion of New Securities, the other Qualified Holders may purchase such portion on a pro rata basis, by giving written notice to the Company within five days from the date that the Company provides written notice to the other Qualified Holders of the amount of New Securities with respect to which such nonpurchasing Qualified Holder has failed to exercise its or his right hereunder.

(d)   If any Qualified Holder or Qualified Holders fail to exercise the foregoing right of first refusal with respect to any New Securities within such twenty (20) day period (or the additional five-day period provided for overallotments), the Company may within one hundred and twenty (120) days thereafter sell any or all of such New Securities not agreed to be purchased by the Qualified Holders, at a price and upon general terms no more favorable to the purchasers thereof than specified in the notice given to each Qualified Holder pursuant to paragraph (c) above. In the event the Company has not sold such New Securities within such one hundred and twenty (120) day period, the Company shall not thereafter issue or sell any New Securities without first offering such New Securities to the Qualified Holders in the manner provided above.

Section 4.21.   <u>Limitation of Option Grants</u>. The Company will not issue or sell more than an aggregate of _____ shares of Common Stock to employees, officers and/or directors of, and/or consultants to, the Company or any subsidiary of the Company pursuant to the exercise of options granted under the Company's stock option plans or pursuant to other stock incentive arrangements (including, but not limited to, so-called "restricted stock").

Section 4.22.   <u>Auditor</u>. The Company shall retain a firm of certified public accountants of established national reputation to audit its books and records at least annually.

Section 4.23.   <u>Negative Covenants</u>. The Company hereby agrees that it will not:

(a)   authorize or issue shares of any class of stock having any preference or priority as to dividends or assets superior to or on a parity with any such preference or priority of the Series A Preferred Stock; increase or decrease the number of directors constituting the Board of Directors of the Company; or reduce the percentage of shares of Series A Preferred Stock required to consent to any of the above matters, or alter or negate the need for such consent;

(b)   reclassify any shares of any class of stock into shares having any preference or priority as to dividends or assets superior to or on a parity with any such preference or priority of the Series A Preferred Stock;

(c)   make any amendment to its Certificate of Incorporation or Bylaws adversely affecting (directly or indirectly) the rights of holders of the Series A Preferred Stock;

(d)   engage in any business other than businesses engaged in or proposed to be engaged in by the Company on the date hereof or businesses similar thereto;

(e)   merge or consolidate with any person or entity (other than mergers of wholly owned subsidiaries into the Company), or sell, lease or otherwise dispose of its assets other than in the ordinary course of business involving an aggregate consideration of more than ten percent (10%) of the book value of its assets on a consolidated basis in any 12-month period, or liquidate, dissolve, recapitalize or reorganize;

(f)   repurchase any shares of its Common Stock from any of its existing stockholders;

(g)   pay dividends or make any other distribution on, or redeem, any shares of any class or series of its equity securities other than the Series A Preferred Stock, unless (a) all dividends accrued on shares of the Series A Preferred Stock shall have been declared and paid, (b) all redemptions of Series A Preferred Stock have occurred in accordance with the schedule set forth in the Certificate of Designation, and (c) the Company's consolidated net worth (determined in accordance with generally accepted accounting principles consistently applied) will be in excess of $_____ immediately after such payment, distribution or redemption;

(h)   enter into any new agreement or make any amendment to any existing agreement, which by its terms would restrict the Company's performance of its obligations to holders of Series A Preferred Stock pursuant to this Agreement or any agreement contemplated hereby;

(i)   enter into any agreement with any holder or prospective holder of any securities of the Company providing for the granting to such holder of registration rights[, preemptive rights, special voting rights or protection against dilution];

(j)   incur any indebtedness for borrowed money or become a guarantor or otherwise contingently liable for any such indebtedness except for trade payables or purchase money obligations incurred in the ordinary course of business; or

>   Comment: *An interesting provision may be bargained for by investors which are C corporations, namely: This provision protects the ability of the Investor C corporation to treat dividends as dividends, and therefore realize the tax benefits flowing from the dividends-received deduction.*

(k)   take any action voluntarily which would require or permit, or could reasonably be expected to require or permit, the Company to treat the dividends on the Shares or any part thereof as deductible interest payments on its books or its federal, state or local income tax returns and shall take no such action which would require or permit, or could reasonably be expected to require or permit, the Company to treat the dividends on the Shares or any part thereof as deductible under any provision of the Code, whether now in effect or hereafter enacted or adopted, unless, in either case, such action would not result in denial of the dividends received deduction presently provided by Section 243(a)(1) of the Code (the "Dividends Received Deduction") or any successor dividends received deduction provided by a similar successor provision of the Code (a "Successor Dividends Received Deduction") to any Holder who would otherwise be eligible to claim such deduction. In addition, the Company shall not take any action voluntarily which could reasonably be expected to cause the Dividends Received Deduction or a Successor Dividends Received Deduction to be eliminated or reduced with respect to dividends on the Shares. The agreements contained in this Section shall be inapplicable if the Code shall be amended after delivery of the Shares in such a manner as to provide that dividends on the Shares may not be treated as dividends for federal income tax purposes or to permit all or a portion of the dividends on the Shares to be deducted by the Company without causing the Dividends Received Deduction or a Successor Dividends Received Deduction to be unavailable to any holder of Shares. This Section shall not be deemed a representation or warranty by the Company that any holder of Shares shall be entitled to the Dividends Received Deduction or any Successor Dividends Received Deduction.

Section 4.24.   Waiver. Any violation of an affirmative or negative covenant of the Company may be waived prospectively or retrospectively in a given instance by a vote of the Investor Directors, but such waiver shall operate only with respect to the particular violation specified in the waiver. The Investor Directors, and the Investors on whose behalf they act, disclaim any intent or purpose to control the Company or to manage its affairs for the benefit of the Investors or otherwise. If deemed advisable, the Investor Directors may elect to delegate the authority to determine the issue of waiver under this Section to a majority of the Investors.

Section 4.25. Termination of Covenants. The covenants of the Company contained in this Section shall terminate, and be of no further force or effect, upon the effective date of a Qualified Public Offering.

ARTICLE V

REPRESENTATIONS AND WARRANTIES OF THE INVESTORS

Each of the Investors severally represents and warrants to the Company, at and as of the Closing that:

Section 5.1. Power and Authority. Such Investor has full power and authority and, if not an individual Investor, has taken all required corporate (or trust or partnership, as the case may be) and other action necessary to permit it to execute and deliver this Agreement, and all other documents or instruments required by this Agreement, and to carry out the terms of this Agreement and of all such other documents or instruments.

Section 5.2. Purchase for Investment. Such Investor is purchasing the Series A Preferred Stock and any Common Stock into which such Series A Preferred Stock may be converted for investment, for its own account and not for the account of any Employee Benefit Plan (or if such Series A Preferred Stock is being acquired for the account of any such Plan, such acquisition does not involve a nonexempt prohibited transaction within the meaning of Section 406 of ERISA or Section 4975 of the Code) and not with a view to distribution thereof, except for transfers permitted hereunder. Such Investor understands that the Series A Preferred Stock and any Common Stock received upon conversion of the Series A Preferred Stock must be held indefinitely unless it is registered under the '33 Act or an exemption from such registration becomes available, and that the Series A Preferred Stock and any Common Stock received upon conversion thereof may only be transferred as provided in this Agreement.

Section 5.3. Financial Matters. Such Investor represents and warrants to the Company that it understands that the purchase of the Shares involves substantial risk and that its financial condition and investments are such that it is in a financial position to hold the Shares for an indefinite period of time and to bear the economic risk of, and withstand a complete loss of, such Shares. In addition, by virtue of its expertise, the advice available to it and previous investment experience, such Investor has extensive knowledge and experience in financial and business matters, investments, securities and private placements and the capability to evaluate the merits and risks of the transactions contemplated by this Agreement. Such Investor represents that it is an "accredited investor" as that term is defined in Regulation D promulgated under the '33 Act.

During the negotiation of the transactions contemplated herein, the Investor and its representatives have been afforded full and free access to corporate books, financial statements, records, contracts, documents, and other information concerning the Company and to its offices and facilities, have been afforded an opportunity to ask such questions of the Company's officers and employees concerning the Company's business, operations, financial condition, assets, liabilities and other relevant matters as they have deemed necessary or desirable, and have been given all such information as has been requested, in order to evaluate the merits and risks of the prospective investment contemplated herein.

Section 5.4.   Brokers, etc. Such Investor has dealt with no broker, finder, commission agent, or other similar person in connection with the offer or sale of the Series A Preferred Stock and the transactions contemplated by this Agreement, and is under no obligation to pay any broker's fee, finder's fee, or commission in connection with such transactions.

Section 5.5.   Subscription Agreements. Such Investor has entered into a subscription agreement [substantially in the form accompanying the Offering Memorandum] and all representations made by such Investor in such agreement are true.

ARTICLE VI

THE CLOSING AND CLOSING CONDITIONS

Section 6.1.   The Closing. The purchase and sale of the Series A Preferred Stock shall take place at the Closing to be held at the offices of _____, located in _____. The Closing shall occur on _____, 199_, or, at the Company's option, such other date not later than _____, 199_, as the Company and a majority in interest of the Investors may designate.

The obligation of each Investor to purchase the Series A Preferred Stock at the Closing shall be subject to satisfaction of the following conditions at and as of the Closing:

Section 6.2.   Issuance of Series A Preferred Stock. The Company shall have duly issued and delivered certificates to each of the Investors for the number of shares of the Series A Preferred Stock purchased by such Investor as provided in Exhibit 2.1.

Section 6.3.   Legal Opinion from Counsel for the Company. There shall be made available to each of the Investors the written opinion of [_____], counsel for the Company, in substantially the form attached as Exhibit 6.3.

The Investors shall have received from [name of Company's counsel] counsel for the Company, a favorable opinion satisfactory to the Investors and your special counsel, dated the date of closing, as to the matters specified in Sections 3.1, 3.2, 3.3.3, 3.5, and 3.6.3, inclusive, and as to: (i) the corporate power of the Company to carry on its business as conducted and as proposed to be conducted; (ii) the due qualification of the Company as a foreign corporation to transact business in, and the good standing of the Company in [City]; (iii) the execution and delivery of this Agreement and the offering and issuance of the Series A Preferred Stock issued at the Closing, the issuance of Common Stock upon conversion of the Series A Preferred Stock, and the fulfillment of and compliance with the respective terms and provisions hereof and thereof, not conflicting with or resulting in a breach of the terms, conditions or provisions of, or constituting a default under, or resulting in any violation of, or requiring any authorization, consent, approval, exemption or other action by or notice to any court or administrative or governmental body pursuant to the certificate of incorporation or bylaws of the Company, any applicable law (except with respect to securities laws vis-à-vis Common Stock issuable upon conversion of the Series A Preferred Stock, as to which such counsel need express no opinion), statute, rule or regulation or (insofar as is known to such counsel after having made due inquiry with respect thereto) any agreement, instrument, order, judgment or decree to which the Company is subject; (iv) the absence of any requirement to register the Series A Preferred Stock being purchased or acquired under the '33 Act, as amended; (v) the authorized and issued capital stock of the Company, including the due and valid issuance, full payment and nonassessability of all issued shares of its capital stock and the compliance of each such issuance with the '33 Act, as amended, and the rules and regulations thereunder; (vi) the due authorization, execution and delivery by each party thereto and the validity of the Agreement; and (vii) such other matters incident to the matters herein contemplated as counsel to the Investors may reasonably request.

Section 6.3.1.   Opinion of Patent Counsel. Each Investor shall have received from _____, patent counsel to the Company, an opinion addressed to it, dated the Closing Date, in the form and substance satisfactory to counsel to the Investors regarding the results of a patent search performed by such counsel and regarding the status of the Company's pending patent applications.

Section 6.4.   Certificate of Officer of the Company. The Company shall have delivered to the Investors a certificate of its chief executive and chief financial officers, or alternatives therefor satisfactory to counsel for the Investors, dated the date of the Closing, to the effect that the representations and warranties of the Company are true at and as of the Closing as if made at and as of the Closing, and that each of the conditions in this Article 6 has been satisfied.

Section 6.5.   Execution of Related Documents. The Company and the Investors shall have duly authorized and executed a Shareholders Agreement in the form set forth as Exhibit 6.5 hereof. [Add here any other agreements to be contemporaneously executed.]

Section 6.6.   Insurance on Certain Key Employees. The Company shall deliver certificates evidencing the policies of life insurance that the Company is required to maintain in force.

Section 6.7.   Employee Documents.   Prior to the Closing, each employee of and consultant to the Company shall have executed an Employee Confidentiality and Noncompetition Agreement.

Section 6.8.   Investor Review. Prior to the Closing, the Investors shall have completed their review of, and shall be satisfied with their conclusions regarding, the Company's markets, business and projected operations.

Section 6.9.   Restated Certificate of Incorporation.   The Restated Certificate shall have been filed with the Secretary of State of Delaware in accordance with Delaware law.

Section 6.10.   Comfort Letter. Each Investor shall have received from _____ , certified public accountants, a letter addressed to it dated the Closing date, in form and substance satisfactory to such Investor, with respect to the Company's results of operations from _____ to _____, and its backlog as of _____.

Section 6.11.   Representations and Warranties to be True and Correct. The representations and warranties contained in Article III shall be true and correct on and as of the Closing Date with the same effect as though such representations and warranties had been made on and as of such date (except to the extent that any representations and warranties of the Company specifically apply to conditions existing at a particular date), and the Company shall have certified to such effect to the Investors in writing.

Section 6.12.   Performance.   The Company shall have performed and complied with all agreements and conditions contained herein required to be performed or complied with by it prior to or at the Closing Date, and the Company shall have certified to such effect to the Investors in writing.

Section 6.13.   All Proceedings to Be Satisfactory.   All corporate and other proceedings to be taken by the Company in connection with the transactions contemplated hereby and all documents incident thereto shall be satisfactory in form and substance to the Investors and their special counsel, and the Investors and said counsel shall have received all such counterpart originals or certified or other copies of such documents as they may reasonably request.

Section 6.14.   Investment by Other Investors.   On the Closing Date, concurrently with the purchase by such Investor, each other Investor shall have purchased and paid for the Series A Preferred Shares being purchased by it hereunder.

Section 6.15.   Supporting Documents.   On or prior to the Closing Date the Investors and their special counsel shall have received copies of the following supporting documents:

(1) (a) copies of the Certificate of Incorporation of the Company, and all amendments thereto, certified as of a recent date by the Secretary of State of the State of Delaware

(b)   a certificate of said Secretary dated as of a recent date as to the due incorporation and good standing of the Company and listing all documents of the Company on file with said Secretary

(c)   a telegram or telex from said Secretary as of the close of business on the next business day preceding the Closing Date as to the continued good standing of the Company

(d)   a certificate of the Secretary or an Assistant Secretary of the Company, dated the Closing Date and certifying: (1) that attached thereto is a true and complete copy of the Bylaws of the Company as in effect on the date of such certification; (2) that attached thereto is a true and complete copy of resolutions adopted by the Board of Directors of the Company authorizing the execution, delivery and performance of this Agreement, the issuance, sale, and delivery of the Series A Preferred Shares, and that all such resolutions are still in full force and effect and are all the resolutions adopted in connection with the transactions contemplated by this Agreement; (3) that the Certificate of Incorporation of the Company has not been amended since the date of the last amendment referred to in the certificate delivered pursuant to clause (b) above; and (4) the incumbency and specimen signature of each officer of the Company executing this Agreement, the stock certificate or certificates representing the Preferred Shares and any certificate or instrument furnished pursuant hereto, and a certification by another officer of the Company as to the incumbency and signature of the officer signing the certificate referred to in this paragraph (d); and

(e) such additional supporting documents and other information with respect to the operations and affairs of the Company as the Investors or their special counsel may reasonably request.

All such documents shall be satisfactory in form and substance to the Investors and their counsel.

Section 6.16. Reasonable Satisfaction of Investors and Counsel. All instruments applicable to the issuance and sale of the Series A Preferred Stock and all proceedings taken in connection with the transactions contemplated by this Agreement shall be reasonably satisfactory to the Investors.

ARTICLE VII

MISCELLANEOUS

Section 7.1. Expenses. The Company and the Investors will each bear their own expenses, including legal fees, in connection with this Agreement. Legal fees incurred by the Investors will be payable by the Company but not in an amount to exceed $_____.

Section 7.2. General Indemnity. Unless the Founders are to make and/or stand behind the Company's representations, warranties and covenants, there is usually not much point in an elaborate indemnification section.

Section 7.3. Remedies Cumulative. Except as herein provided, the remedies provided herein shall be cumulative and shall not preclude assertion by any party hereto of any other rights or the seeking of any other remedies against the other party hereto.

Section 7.4.   <u>Certain Fees and Expenses</u>. If the Investors shall employ counsel for advice or other representation or shall incur legal or other costs and expenses in connection with (i) any amendment or modification proposed by the Company of this Agreement, the Certificate of Incorporation of the Company or the Registration Rights Agreement, or (ii) any litigation, contest, dispute, suit, proceeding or action instituted by the Investors or any of them, in respect to the enforcement of the Investors' rights under this Agreement, or the Shareholders Agreement, then, and in any such event, the attorneys' fees arising from such services and all expenses, costs, charges and other fees of such counsel incurred in connection with or related to any of the events or actions described above shall be payable by the Company.

Section 7.5.   <u>Brokerage</u>. Each party hereto will indemnify and hold harmless the others against and in respect of any claim for brokerage or other commission relative to this Agreement or to the transaction contemplated hereby, based in any way on agreements, arrangements or understandings made or claimed to have been made by such party with any third party.

Section 7.6.   <u>Severability</u>. Whenever possible, each provision of this Agreement shall be interpreted in such a manner as to be effective and valid under applicable law, but if any provision of this Agreement shall be prohibited by or invalid under applicable law, such provisions shall be ineffective to the extent of such prohibition or invalidity, without invalidating the remainder of such provision or the remaining provisions of this Agreement.

Section 7.7.   <u>Parties in Interest</u>. All covenants and agreements contained in this Agreement by or on behalf of any of the parties hereto shall bind and inure to the benefit of the respective legal representatives, successors and assigns of the parties hereto whether so expressed or not.

Section 7.8.   <u>Notices</u>. Notices required under this Agreement shall be deemed to have been adequately given if delivered in person or sent by certified mail, return receipt requested, to the recipient at its address set forth in <u>Exhibit 7.8</u> or such other address as such party may from time to time designate in writing.

Section 7.9.   <u>No Waiver</u>. No failure to exercise and no delay in exercising any right, power or privilege granted under this Agreement shall operate as a waiver of such right, power or privilege. No single or partial exercise of any right, power or privilege granted under this Agreement shall preclude any other or further exercise thereof or the exercise of any other right, power or privilege. The rights and remedies provided in this Agreement are cumulative and are not exclusive of any rights or remedies provided by law.

Section 7.10. <u>Amendments and Waivers</u>. Except as herein provided, this Agreement may be modified or amended only by a writing signed by the Company and by the Holders of sixty-six and two thirds percent (66 2/3%) of the Series A Preferred Stock (the "Required Majority"). Each Investor acknowledges that by the operation of <u>Section 7.10</u> hereof the holders of sixty-six and two thirds percent (66 2/3%) of the outstanding Series A Preferred Stock (and Common Stock issued upon conversion thereof) will have the right and power to diminish or eliminate all rights of such Investor under this Agreement.

Section 7.11. <u>Rights of Investors</u>. Each holder of Series A Preferred Stock (and Common Stock issued upon conversion thereof) shall have the absolute right to exercise or refrain from exercising any right or rights that such holder may have by reason of this Agreement or any Series A Preferred Stock, including without limitation the right to consent to the waiver of any obligation of the Company under this Agreement and to enter into an agreement with the Company for the purpose of modifying this Agreement or any agreement effecting any such modification, and such holder shall not incur any liability to any other holder or holders of Series A Preferred Stock with respect to exercising or refraining from exercising any such right or rights.

Section 7.12. <u>Survival of Agreements, etc</u>. All agreements, representations and warranties contained in this Agreement or made in writing by or on behalf of the Company (and Founders) or the Investors in connection with the transactions contemplated by this Agreement shall survive the execution and delivery of this Agreement, the Closing, and any investigation at any time made by or on behalf of any Investor. Notwithstanding the preceding sentence, however, all such representations (other than intentional misrepresentations) and warranties, but no such agreements, shall expire three years after the date of this Agreement.

Section 7.13. <u>Construction</u>. This Agreement shall be governed by and construed in accordance with the procedural and substantive laws of the State of New York without regard for its conflicts-of-laws rules. The Company agrees that it may be served with process in the State of New York and any action for breach of this Agreement prosecuted against it in the courts of that State.

Section 7.14. <u>Entire Understanding</u>. This Agreement expresses the entire understanding of the parties and supersedes all prior and contemporaneous agreements and undertakings of the parties with respect to the subject matter of this Agreement.

Section 7.15. <u>Counterparts</u>. This Agreement may be executed in one or more counterparts, each of which shall be deemed to be an original but all of which taken together shall constitute one agreement.

Section 7.16.   Remedies. For the purposes of this Agreement, if default shall be made in the due and punctual performance or observance of any term contained in this Agreement or the Company shall violate any of the negative covenants set forth in Section 4.23 of this Agreement, and such default or violation shall have continued for a period of fifteen (15) days after written notice thereof to the Company by the holder of any Shares, an Event of Default shall be deemed to have occurred; provided, however, that the rights and obligations set forth in Article IV hereof shall terminate and no Event of Default shall occur or continue after there has been a Qualified Public Offering.

Section 7.16.1.   Remedy Upon Events of Default. Upon the occurrence of an Event of Default as herein defined, and so long as such Event of Default continues unremedied, then, unless such Event of Default shall have been waived in the manner provided in Section 4.24 hereof, the holders of the Series A Preferred Stock shall be entitled to elect a majority of the Board of Directors in the manner provided in the Articles.

That new Board of Directors may, in addition to all other action taken by the Board of Directors pursuant to the laws of the State of Delaware, the Certificate of Incorporation and Bylaws of the Company:

(a)   sell or otherwise dispose of all or substantially all of the assets of the Company and wind up the affairs of the Company; or

(b)   adopt a new business plan including the change of purpose and objectives of the Company and pursue such business plan.

Section 7.17.   Assignment; No Third-Party Beneficiaries.

(a)   This Agreement and the rights hereunder shall not be assignable or transferable by the Investors or the Company except in the case of an Investor, in accordance with the restrictions on transfer set out in [identify location of restrictions if any] or in the case of the Company by operation of law in connection with a merger, consolidation or sale of substantially all the assets of the Company without the prior written consent of the other parties hereto. Subject to the preceding sentence, this Agreement shall be binding upon, inure to the benefit of and be enforceable by the parties hereto and their respective successors and assigns. The assignment by either Investor on a nonexclusive basis of any rights under this Agreement to any such transferee shall not affect or diminish the rights or obligations of such Buyer under this Agreement and in no event shall any assignment relieve either Investor of its obligations hereunder.

(b)   Except as provided in Section 7.19(a), this Agreement is for the sole benefit of the parties hereto and their permitted assigns and nothing herein expressed or implied shall give or be construed to give to any Person, other than the parties hereto and such assigns, any legal or equitable rights hereunder.

ARTICLE VIII

TERMINATION

Section 8.1.   Termination. This Agreement may be terminated at any time prior to the Closing:

(a)   by mutual consent of the Required Majority and the Company;

(b)   by either the Company or the Required Majority if the Closing shall not have occurred by [Month] [Day], 1996, provided that the failure to consummate the transactions contemplated hereby is not a result of the failure by the party so electing to terminate this Agreement to perform any of its obligations hereunder.

Section 8.2.   Effect of Termination. Except for the obligations of Section 4.1(g) hereof, if this Agreement shall be terminated pursuant to Section 8.1, all obligations, representations and warranties of the parties hereto under the Agreement shall terminate and there shall be no liability, except for any breach of this Agreement prior to such termination, of any party to another party.

ARTICLE IX

ARBITRATION

If at any time there shall be a dispute arising out of or relating to any provision of this Agreement or any agreement contemplated hereby, such dispute shall be submitted for binding and final determination by arbitration in accordance with the regulations then obtaining of the American Arbitration Association. Judgment upon the award rendered by the arbitrator(s) resulting from such arbitration shall be in writing, and shall be final and binding upon all involved parties. The site of any arbitration shall be within [City], [State].

IN WITNESS WHEREOF, the parties hereto have executed this Agreement under seal as of the date first above written.

NEWCO, INC.

By_____
President

Investors:

_____

_____

Founders:

_____

_____

SHAREHOLDERS AGREEMENT

NEWCO, INC.

TABLE OF CONTENTS

SHAREHOLDERS AGREEMENT

SHAREHOLDERS AGREEMENT, dated as of _____, 199_, by and among NEWCO, Inc., a Delaware corporation (the "Company"), the investors listed on Schedule A hereto (collectively the "Investors" and individually an "Investor"), and those existing holders (collectively the "Founders") of the Company's outstanding $.01 par value per share common stock (the "Common Stock") who appear on Schedule B hereto (the Investors and the Founders sometimes hereinafter collectively referred to herein as the "Shareholders" or individually as the "Shareholder").

Comment: *Consider whether the execution of this agreement will enhance the chances a court will find the parties have entered into a partnership or, if not, have undertaken fiduciary duties (as quasi partners) vis a vis each other.*

PREAMBLE

The Investors are purchasing shares of the Company's Series A Cumulative Convertible Preferred Stock, $.01 par value per share (the "Series A Preferred Stock") pursuant to that certain Stock Purchase Agreement of an even date herewith between the Company and the Investors (the "Agreement"), and the Founders hold shares of Common Stock of the Company in the proportions set forth on Schedule B; and

Comment: *Consider whether under state law, all shareholders must execute the agreement and/or be offered an opportunity to sign.*

One of the conditions to the Closing as defined in the Agreement is the execution [by the holders of X% of the outstanding Series Preferred Stock and Y% of outstanding common stock] of this Agreement;

Comment: *If the instant agreement replaces an earlier agreement (as in a subsequent round) then the preamble reads as follows:*

[Certain of the Investors hold shares of the Company's Series A Preferred Stock (the "Series A Preferred Stock") and/or shares of Common Stock issued upon conversion thereof and possess registration rights, information rights, rights of first offer, and other rights pursuant to a Shareholders Agreement dated as of _____, between the Company and such Investors (the "Prior Agreement").

The undersigned Investors who hold Series A Preferred Stock desire to terminate the Prior Agreement and to accept the rights created pursuant hereto in lieu of the rights granted to them under the Prior Agreement.]

NOW, THEREFORE, in consideration of the mutual covenants and agreements contained herein and other good and valuable consideration, the receipt and sufficiency of which are hereby acknowledged, the parties hereto agree as follows:

ARTICLE I

ELECTION OF DIRECTORS

1.1   <u>Election of Directors</u>. At each annual meeting of the stockholders of the Company, or at each special meeting of the stockholders of the Company involving the election of directors of the Company, and at any other time at which stockholders of the Company will have the right to or will vote for or render consent in writing regarding the election of directors of the Company, then and in each event, the Shareholders hereby covenant and agree to vote all shares of capital stock of the Company presently owned or hereafter required by them (whether owned of record or over which any person exercises voting control) in favor of the following actions:

(a)   to fix and maintain the number of directors at seven (7);

(b)   to cause and maintain the election to the Board of Directors of the Company Directors as specified below:

(i)   so long as the Investors hold forty percent (40%) or more of the aggregate voting rights of the Series A Preferred Stock and Common Stock, the Investor shall be entitled to elect that number of directors that is the lowest number that constitutes a majority of the members of the Board of Directors, and the Founders shall be entitled to elect the remaining members of the Board of Directors.

(ii)   so long as the Investors hold twenty percent (20%) or more, but less than forty percent (40%) of the aggregate voting rights of the Series A Preferred Stock and Common Stock, the Investors shall have the right to elect that number of directors that is one person lower than the lowest number that constitutes a majority of the members of the Board of Directors, and the remaining directors shall be elected by the Investors and the Founders voting together.

(iii)   [So long as the Investors elect directors, at least one of such directors elected by the Investors shall be [name of person who is not related to the Company or the Investors in any way] (the "Outside Director)].

Comment: *This language assumes complete identity between "Investors" and holders of Series A Preferred Stock," as those categories of shareholder are defined in the Shareholders Agreement on the one hand and the Stock Purchase Agreement and Certificate of Designation. If these are not identical, this document should be altered to reflect those differences (for example, "if some Investors hold both preferred and common stock, the Investor Directors should be renamed the "Series A Directors," elected by the holders of Series A Preferred Stock alone).*

Comment: *If one of the social covenants involves some degree of employee participation in the management of the Company, this is an appropriate place to provide for the election of at least one employee director. An alternative to the scheme proposed here would be to provide for cumulative* voting, *then allocate shares to the respective parties such that they are in fact able to elect the designated number of directors without any sort of voting agreement. The problems with that approach is that the results are less certain and the future issuance of stock must be undertaken with care to avoid upsetting the voting balance. Alternatively, the board could be divided into different classes of directors, each elected by a holders of a different class or series of stock. This would require the issuance of multiple series of stock. Both of these alternatives help avoid at least some of the fuzziness surrounding the fiduciary obligations of appointed directors to stockholders they do not represent, as in each case, the stockholders will be electing their representatives. However, those obligations extend for the director to all shareholders, and not just those that elected him or her. See Treatise § 10.11. An additional issue to keep in mind is the variation in state law governing the duration of voting agreements (many states limit them to ten years).*

None of the parties entitled to designate directors hereunder shall vote to remove either the Outside Director or any director designated by any other party or group of shareholders pursuant hereto, except for bad faith or willful misconduct. Each of the parties hereto shall vote or cause to be voted all shares owned by them or over which they have voting control (i) to remove from the Board of Directors any director designated by any party pursuant hereto at the request of such party and (ii) to fill any vacancy in the membership of the Board of Directors with a designee of the party whose designee's resignation or removal from the Board caused such vacancy.

1.2   Resignation of Directors. Concurrently with the consummation of a sale of substantially all the Shares owned by either the Investors or the Founders, the sellers shall deliver the resignations of the member(s) of the board of directors of the Company which are represented by such seller's interest.

The Company shall provide to each party entitled to designate directors hereunder prior written notice of any intended mailing of notice to stockholders for a meeting at which directors are to be elected, and any party entitled to designate directors pursuant hereto shall notify the Company in writing, prior to such mailing, of the person(s) designated by it or them as its or their nominee(s) for election as director(s).

The Investor Directors shall be selected by holders of a majority of the outstanding stock owned by the Investors, equating for this purpose Common Stock with the shares of Common Stock owned by the holders of Series A Preferred Stock as if such Preferred Stock were than converted.

If any party entitled to designate directors hereunder fails to give notice to the Company as provided above, it shall be deemed that the designee of such party then serving as director shall be its designee for reelection.

Each party entitled to designate directors hereunder hereby agrees that the Company shall not have any executive or similar committee of the Board of Directors unless the Board of Directors unanimously consents to the formation of such committee.

If the Outside Director shall cease to serve for any reason, the Shareholders will negotiate in good faith a replacement for the Outside Director and, failing agreement, the Outside Director's replacement shall be designated by the majority of the Shareholders.

> Comment: *Certain investors shy away from board seats, Treatise § 9.2, in favor of attendance rights, as follows (these rights may also be secured through the Stock Purchase Agreement, under the affirmative covenants of the Company):*

1.3   Observer Rights. As long as the Investors own not less than five percent (5%) of the aggregate voting rights of the Series A Preferred Stock and Common Stock, the Company shall invite a representative of the Investors to attend all meetings of its Board of Directors in a nonvoting observer capacity and, in this respect, shall give such representative copies of all notices, minutes, consents and other materials it provides to its directors; provided, however, that such representative shall agree to hold in confidence and trust and to act in a fiduciary manner with respect to all information so provided; and, provided further, that the Company reserves the right to withhold any information and to exclude such representative from any meeting or portion thereof if access to such information or attendance at such meeting could adversely affect the attorney-client privilege between the Company and its counsel. The representative of the Investors shall be designated by the majority of the Investors.

ARTICLE II

RIGHT OF CO-SALE

If any Founder proposes to sell any Shares ("Co-Sale Shares") to a party or affiliated group (the "Transferee") in a transaction or series of related transactions involving the sale of more than [   ] Shares or resulting in the Transferee for the first time controlling the power to vote more than fifty percent (50%) of the total votes for nominees to the Company's board of directors, such Founder shall first give reasonable notice in reasonable detail to each Investor in sufficient time to allow each Investor to participate in the sale on the same terms and conditions as such Founder. To the extent any prospective purchaser or purchasers refuses to purchase shares or other securities from an Investor exercising its rights of co-sale hereunder, the Founder shall not sell to such prospective purchaser or purchasers any Shares unless and until, simultaneously with such sale, the Founder shall purchase the offered shares or other securities from the Investor. Notwithstanding the foregoing, the provisions of Article II shall not apply to (i) any pledge of Co-Sale Shares made pursuant to a bona fide loan transaction that creates a mere security interest; (ii) any transfer to the ancestors, descendants or spouse or to trusts for the benefit of such persons of a Founder; or (iii) any bona fide gift; provided that (A) the transferring Founder shall inform the Investors of such pledgee, transfer or gift prior to effecting it and (B) the pledgee, transferee or donee shall furnish the Investors with a written agreement to be bound by and comply with all provisions of Article II. Such transferred Co-Sale Shares will remain "Co-Sale Shares" hereunder, and such pledgee, transferee or donee shall be treated as a "Founder" for purposes of this Agreement.

Notwithstanding the foregoing, the provisions of Article II shall not apply to the sale of any Co-Sale Shares to the public pursuant to a registration statement filed with, and declared effective by, the Securities and Exchange Commission under the Securities Act of 1933, as amended (the "Securities Act"); or (ii) to the Company.

In the event of a conflict between the Investors' right of Co-Sale hereunder and the provisions, either in an agreement or the Company's certificate of incorporation, requiring the Investor to offer Shares prior to sale to the Company or a third party ("Restrictions on Transfer"), the right of Co-Sale shall control. Nothing in this paragraph shall, however, diminish the Founders' first refusal obligations under such restrictions on Transfer.

ARTICLE III

"DRAG-ALONG" RIGHTS

If at any time any one or more of the Shareholders (the "Seller(s)") shall propose to undertake a sale of fifty percent (50%) or more of the Company's then issued and outstanding shares of capital stock to a single Person in a single transaction or series of related transactions (a "Proposed Transaction"), then each Shareholder shall, if requested by such Seller(s), sell all of his Shares in such transaction on the same terms and for the same consideration. Such Seller(s) shall give each Shareholder written notice of any Proposed Transaction at least twenty (20) days prior to the date on which such transaction shall be consummated, including the terms and conditions thereof, and each Shareholder shall have the obligation to sell his Shares on such same terms and conditions in accordance with the instructions set forth in such notice. In such event, each Shareholder shall deliver the Share certificate(s) (accompanied by duly executed stock powers or other instrument of transfer duly endorsed in blank) representing the Shares to the Company or to an agent designated by the Company, for the purpose of effectuating the transfer of the Shares to the purchaser and the disbursement of the proceeds of such transactions to the Shareholder(s). The Company may, at its option, deposit the consideration payable for the Shares with a depository designated by it and thereafter each Share certificate shall represent only the right to receive the consideration payable in the transaction.

> Comment: *If the primary exit strategy of the Investor(s) is through the sale of the Company, this provision may be critical to accomplishing that sale in a timely manner, as timely is defined by the Investor. It may be important enough that the right to compel the sale of the Company (through the exercise of drag-along rights to force other, minority shareholders to sell alongside the Investor(s)) should be specifically reserved for the Investor(s). While the provision may not itself be that practically useful, it will provide the Investor(s) with leverage against a complacent yet ineffectual management team reluctant to aggressively seek a buyer for the Company. These drag-along rights may be of questionable legal enforceability, as they enable the majority to impose a critical decision on the minority without provision for appraisal and other dissenter's rights; rights that are typically available in the event of a merger or other major event, yet have essentially been drafted away by this agreement. Delaware*

courts have, in at least one instance (and in dictum) indicated a willingness to uphold such a provision, see Shields v. Shields, 498 A.2d 161, 168 (Del. Ch. 1985). It is not clear how other state courts, or even how Delaware itself, will treat such agreements in the future. Precise drafting is thus imperative. See generally, Treatise § 10.15.

ARTICLE IV

RESTRICTIONS ON TRANSFER

Comment: *Some provisions restricting transfer are contained in the model certificate of incorporation. For more detailed provisions, see "Provisions Governing Restrictions on Transfer."*

4.1   The following restrictions are imposed upon the transfer of shares of the capital stock of the Company:

The Company shall have the right to purchase, or to direct the transfer of, the shares of its capital stock in the events and subject to the conditions and at a price fixed as provided below. Each holder of shares of such capital stock holds his shares subject to this right and by accepting the same upon original issuance or subsequent transfer thereof, the holder agrees for himself, his legal representatives and assigns as follows:

In the event of any change in the ownership of any share or shares of such capital stock (made or proposed) or in the right to vote thereon (whether by the holder's act or by death, legal disability, operation of law, legal processes, order of court, or otherwise, except by ordinary proxies or powers of attorney), the Company has the right to purchase all or any part of such shares or to require the same to be sold to a purchaser or purchasers designated by the Company, or to follow each such method in part, at a price per share equal to the fair value thereof at the close of business on the last business day next preceding such event as determined by mutual agreement or, failing such agreement, by arbitration as provided below. Fair value, for this purpose, shall be determined as if the Company was being sold to an unaffiliated third party as an entry, with no discount applied to the shares by reason of illiquidity or minority position.

In any such event the owner of the share or shares concerned therein (being, for the purposes of these provisions, all persons having any actual or inchoate property interest therein) shall give notice thereof in detail satisfactory to the Company. Within ten (10) days after receipt of said owner's notice, the Company shall elect whether or not to exercise its said rights in respect to said shares and, if it elects to exercise them, shall give notice of its election.

Failing agreement between the owner and the Company as to the price per share to be paid, such price shall be the fair value of such shares as determined by three (3) arbitrators, one designated within five (5) days after the termination of said ten (10) day period by the registered holder of said share or shares or his legal representatives, one within said period of (5) five days by the Company, and the third within five (5) days after said appointment last occurring by the two (2) so chosen. Successor arbitrators, if any shall be required, shall be appointed, within reasonable time, as nearly as may be in the manner provided as to the related original appointment. No appointment shall be deemed as having been accomplished unless such arbitrator shall have accepted in writing his appointment as such within the time limited for his appointment. Notice of each appointment of an arbitrator shall be given promptly to the other parties in interest. Said arbitrators shall proceed promptly to determine said fair value. The determination of the fair value of said share or shares by agreement of any two (2) of the arbitrators shall be conclusive upon all parties interested in such shares. Forthwith upon such determination the arbitrators shall mail or deliver notice of such determination to the owner (as above defined) and to the Company. The reasonable fees and expenses of the arbitrators shall be paid by the Company.

Within ten (10) days after agreement upon said price or mailing of notice of determination of said price by the arbitrators as provided above (whichever shall last occur), the shares specified therein for purchase shall be transferred to the Company or to the purchaser or purchasers designated therein or in part to each as indicated in such notice of election against payment of said price at the principal office of the Company.

If in any of the said events, notice therefor having been given as provided above, the Company elects in respect of any such shares or any part thereof not to exercise its said rights, or fails to exercise them or to give notice or make payment, all as provided above, or waives said rights by vote or in authorized writing, then such contemplated transfer or such change may become effective as to those shares with respect to which the Company elects not to exercise its rights or fails to exercise them or to give notice or to make payment, if consummated within thirty (30)days after such election, failure or waiver by the Company, or within such longer period as the Company may authorize.

If the owner's notice in respect of any of such shares of capital stock is not received by the Company as provided above, or if the owner fails to comply with these provisions in respect of any such shares in any other regard, the Company, at its option and in addition to its other remedies, may suspend the rights to vote or to receive dividends on said shares, or may refuse to register on its books any transfer of said shares or otherwise to recognize any transfer or change in the ownership thereof or in the right to vote thereon, one or more, until these provisions are complied with to the satisfaction of the Company; and if the required owner's notice is not received by the Company after written demand by the Company, it may also or independently proceed as though a proper owner's notice had been received at the expiration of ten days after mailing such demand, and, if it exercises its rights with respect to said shares or any of them, the shares specified shall be transferred, and/or deemed transferred, accordingly.

In respect of these provisions, the Company may act by its Board of Directors, not including the vote of any director personally interested in the transfer. Any notice or demand under said provisions shall be deemed to have been sufficiently given if in writing, delivered by hand or addressed by mail postpaid, to the Company at its principal office or to the owner (as above defined) or to the holder registered on the books of the Company (or his legal representative) of the share or shares in question at the address stated in his notice or at his address appearing on the books of the Company. Nothing herein contained shall prevent the pledging of shares if there is neither a transfer of the legal title thereto nor a transfer on the books of the Company into the name of the pledgee. But no pledgee or person claiming thereunder shall be entitled to make or cause to be made any transfer of pledged shares by sale thereof or otherwise (including in this prohibition transfers on the books of the Company into the name of the pledgee) except upon compliance herewith, and any such pledge shall be subject to those conditions and restrictions.

> Comment: *In Form 1.00, Article Fourth, the Company enjoys a right of first option, meaning that any attempted transfer (voluntary or not) gives rise to a right in the Company to call away the stock at a set or arbitrated price. A right of first refusal or first offer applies only to voluntary transfers, the Company and/or the other shareholders enjoying the right to match a third party offer.*

ARTICLE V

RIGHT OF FIRST OFFER

> Comment: *This is a preemptive right.*

Subject to the terms and conditions specified in this <u>Article V</u>, the Company hereby grants to each Major Investor (as hereinafter defined) a right of first offer with respect to future sales by the Company of its Shares (as hereinafter defined). For purposes of this <u>Article V</u>, a Major Investor shall mean (i) any Investor who holds at least ten percent (10%) of the original investment such Investor made in the Company pursuant to this Agreement and (ii) any person who acquires at least ten percent (10%) of the Series A Preferred Stock (or the Common Stock issued upon conversion thereof) issued pursuant to this Agreement. (For purposes of this <u>Article V</u> "Investor" includes any general partners and/or affiliates of an Investor. An Investor shall be entitled to apportion the right of first offer hereby granted it among itself and its partners and affiliates in such proportions as it deems appropriate.)

Each time the Company proposes to offer any shares of, or securities convertible into or exercisable for any shares of, any class or its capital stock ("Shares"), the Company shall first make an offering of such Shares to each Major Investor in accordance with the following provisions:

(a)   The Company shall deliver a notice by certified mail ("Notice") to the Major Investors stating (i) its bona fide intention to offer such Shares, (ii) the number of such Shares to be offered, and (iii) the price and terms, if any, upon which it proposes to offer such Shares.

(b)   Within twenty (20) calendar days after [receipt] [giving] of the Notice, each Major Investor may elect to purchase or obtain, at the price and on the terms specified in the Notice, up to that portion of such Shares which equals the proportion that the number of shares of Common Stock issued and held, or issuable upon conversion of the Series A Preferred Stock then held, by such Major Investor bears to the total number of shares of Common Stock issued and held, or issuable upon conversion of the Series A Preferred Stock then held, by all the Major Investors. The Company shall promptly, in writing, inform each Major Investor which purchases all the shares available to it ("Fully-Exercising Investor") of any other Major Investor's failure to do likewise. During the ten-day period commencing after [receipt of] such information is given, each Fully-Exercising Investor shall be entitled to obtain that portion of the Shares not subscribed for by the Major Investors equal to the proportion the number of shares of Common Stock issued and held, or issuable upon conversion of Series A Preferred Stock then held, by such Fully-Exercising Investor bears to the total number of shares of Common Stock issued and held, or issuable upon conversion of the Series A Preferred Stock then held, by all Fully-Exercising Investors who wish to purchase some of the unsubscribed shares.

(c)   If all Shares are not elected to be obtained as provided in Article V(b), the Company may, during the thirty (30) day period following the expiration of the period provided in Article V(b) hereof, offer the remaining unsubscribed portion of such Shares to any person or persons at a price not less than, and upon terms no more favorable to the offeree than those specified in the Notice. If the Company does not enter into an agreement for the sale of the Shares within such period, or if such agreement is not consummated within thirty (30) days of the execution thereof, the right provided hereunder shall be deemed to be revived and such Shares shall not be offered unless first reoffered to the Major Investors in accordance herewith.

The right of first offer in this Article V shall not be applicable (i) to the issuance or sale of not to exceed _____ Shares of Common Stock (or options therefor) to employees or (ii) to or after consummation of a bona fide, firmly underwritten public offering of shares of common stock, registered under the Act pursuant to a registration statement on Form S-1, at an offering price of at least $_____ per share (appropriately adjusted for any stock split, dividend, combination or other recapitalization) [and $_____ in the aggregate] or [, (iii) the issuance of securities pursuant to the conversion or exercise of convertible or exercisable securities, or (iv) the issuance of securities in connection with a bona fide business acquisition of or by the Company, whether by merger, consolidation, sale of assets, sale or exchange of stock or otherwise, or (v) the issuance of stock, warrants or other securities or rights to persons or entities with which the Company has business relationships [provided such issuances are for other than primarily equity financing purposes and] [provided that at the time of any such issuance, the aggregate of such issuance and similar issuances in the preceding twelve (12) month period do not exceed two percent (2%) of the then outstanding Common Stock of the Company (assuming full conversion and exercise of all convertible and exercisable securities)]].

ARTICLE VI

MANAGEMENT AND CONTROL

6.1   General.   The business and affairs of the Company shall be managed, controlled and operated in accordance with its certificate of incorporation and by-laws, as the same may be amended from time to time, except that neither the certificate of incorporation nor the by-laws shall be amended in any manner that would conflict with, or be inconsistent with, the provisions of this Agreement.

6.2   Limitation on Certain Actions by the Company.   Without the prior affirmative vote of the holders in interest of two-thirds of the Series A Preferred Stock then outstanding, the Company shall not:

(a)   adopt or effect any plan of sale, merger, consolidation, dissolution, reorganization or recapitalization of the Company;

(b)   offer for sale or sell all or substantially all of the assets of the Company; or

(c)   issue, sell or deliver any capital stock, or any interest therein, of the Company; or

(d)   amend or restate the Company's certificate of incorporation or by-laws.

ARTICLE VII

MISCELLANEOUS

7.1   <u>Transfer of Stock</u>. Except as otherwise expressly provided by this Agreement, each Shareholder agrees not to transfer any of his or her shares of capital stock of the Company unless the transferee agrees in writing to be bound by the terms and conditions of this Agreement and executes a counterpart of this Agreement, and unless such Shareholder has complied with applicable law in connection with such transfer.

7.2   <u>Duration of Agreement</u>. The rights and obligations of the Company and each Shareholder under this Agreement shall terminate on the earliest to occur of the following: (a) immediately prior to the consummation of the first underwritten public offering by the Company pursuant to an effective registration statement under the Securities Act of 1933 of any of its equity securities for its own account in which the aggregate gross proceeds to the Company equal or exceed $5,000,000, or when the Company first becomes subject to the periodic reporting requirements of Section 12(g) or 15(d) of the 1934 Act, whichever event shall first occur, (b) immediately prior to the consummation of the sale of all, or substantially all, of the Company's assets or capital stock or a merger, consolidation, reorganization or other business combination of the Company which results in the transfer of more than fifty percent (50%) of the voting securities of the Company, or (c) the tenth anniversary hereof.

Comment: *The language about the Company becoming public covers Non-IPO events such as a public sale of stock under Regulation A or the use of the reverse acquisition technique.*

Comment: *On occasion, termination is conditioned on the underwriting achieving a certain price per share, meaning a "step up" from the investors' price. Care must be taken to achieve an "apples to apples" comparison since many IPOs entail a stock or reverse stock split.*

7.3   Legend. Each certificate representing shares of Series A Preferred Stock and Common Stock shall bear the following legend, until such time as the shares of Series A Preferred Stock and Common Stock represented thereby are no longer subject to the provisions hereof:

"THE SALE, TRANSFER OR ASSIGNMENT OF THE SECURITIES REPRESENTED BY THIS CERTIFICATE ARE SUBJECT TO THE TERMS AND CONDITIONS OF A CERTAIN SHAREHOLDERS AGREEMENT DATED _____, 199_, AMONG THE COMPANY AND HOLDERS OF ITS OUTSTANDING CAPITAL STOCK. COPIES OF SUCH AGREEMENT MAY BE OBTAINED AT NO COST BY WRITTEN REQUEST MADE BY THE HOLDER OF RECORD OF THIS CERTIFICATE TO THE SECRETARY OF THE COMPANY."

7.4   Severability; Governing Law. If any provisions of this Agreement shall be determined to be illegal or unenforceable by any court of law, the remaining provisions shall be severable and enforceable in accordance with their terms. This Agreement shall be governed by, and construed in accordance with, the internal laws of the State of [_____].

7.5   Insider Transactions. The Company and the Shareholders agree that any transactions between the Company and its officers, directors, principal Shareholders or their affiliates, including, without limitation, any sales of capital stock or assets of the Company, will be on terms no less favorable to the Company than could be obtained from unaffiliated third parties on an arm's length basis and will require the approval of a majority of the Company's disinterested directors.

Comment: *This language pops up from time to time. It can be troublesome, particularly if some of the stockholders buy additional stock in a burn out or cram down transaction. See Treatise §21.2(a)(ii).*

7.6   Injunctive Relief. It is acknowledged that it will be impossible to measure the damages that would be suffered by the non-breaching party if any party fails to comply with the provisions of this Agreement and that in the event of any such failure, the non-breaching parties will not have an adequate remedy at law. The non-breaching parties shall, therefore, be entitled to obtain specific performance of the breaching party's obligations hereunder and to obtain immediate injunctive relief. The breaching party shall not urge, as a defense to any proceeding for such specific performance or injunctive relief, that the non-breaching parties have an adequate remedy at law.

If any action at law or in equity is necessary to enforce or interpret the terms of this Agreement, the prevailing party shall be entitled to reasonable attorneys' fees, costs and necessary disbursements in addition to any other relief to which such party may be entitled.

7.7   Binding Effect. This Agreement shall be binding upon and inure to the benefit of the parties hereto and their respective permitted successors and assignees, legal representatives and heirs. Nothing in this Agreement, express or implied, is intended to confer upon any party other than the parties hereto or their respective successors and assigns any rights, remedies, obligations, or liabilities under or by reason of this Agreement, except as expressly provided in this Agreement. The administrator, executor or legal representative of any deceased, juvenile or incapacitated Shareholder shall have the right to execute and deliver all documents and perform all acts necessary to exercise and perform the rights and obligations of such Shareholder under the terms of this Agreement.

7.8   Modification or Amendment. Neither this Agreement nor any provisions hereof can be modified, amended, changed, discharged or terminated except by an instrument in writing, signed by the Shareholders of at least a majority of the shares of capital stock then subject to this Agreement held by such Shareholders, based upon voting power and calculated on an "as if converted" basis, together with the consent of Investors holding at least a majority of the outstanding shares of Series A Preferred Stock.

7.9   Counterparts. This Agreement may be executed in one or more counterparts, each of which shall be deemed to be an original, but all of which taken together shall constitute one and the same instrument.

7.10   Notices. All notices to be given or otherwise made to any party to this Agreement shall be deemed to be sufficient if contained in a written instrument, delivered by hand in person, or by express overnight courier service, or by electronic facsimile transmission (with a copy sent by first class mail, postage prepaid), or by registered or certified mail, return receipt requested, postage prepaid, addressed to such party at the address set forth herein or at such other address as may hereafter be designated in writing by the addressee to the addressor listing all parties.

All such notices shall, when mailed or telegraphed, be effective when received or when attempted delivery is refused.

7.11   <u>No Other Agreements</u>.   Each Shareholder represents that he has not granted and is not a party to any proxy, voting trust or other agreement which is inconsistent with or conflicts with the provisions of this Agreement, and no holder of Shares shall grant any proxy or become party to any voting trust or other agreement which is inconsistent with or conflicts with the provisions of this Agreement.

7.12   <u>Certificate of Incorporation and By-laws</u>.   The certificate of incorporation and by-laws of the Company may be amended in any manner permitted thereunder, except that neither the certificate nor the by-laws shall be amended in any manner that would conflict with, or be inconsistent with, the provisions of this Agreement.

7.13   <u>IRC Section 305</u>.   So long as any shares of Series A Preferred Stock remain outstanding, the Company will not, without approval of holders of a majority of the Series A Preferred Stock then outstanding, do any act or thing which would result in taxation of the holders of shares of the Series A Preferred Stock under Section 305 of the Internal Revenue Code of 1986, as amended (or any comparable provision of the Internal Revenue Code as hereafter from time to time amended).

<u>Comment</u>: *See Treatise §13.6*

7.14   <u>Aggregation of Stock</u>.   All shares of the Preferred Stock held or acquired by affiliated entities or persons shall be aggregated together for the purpose of determining the availability of any rights under this Agreement.

IN WITNESS WHEREOF, the Company, the Investors and the Founders have executed this agreement in counterparts as of the date first above specified.

NEWCO, INC.

By: _____
President

Investors:

_____

_____

Founders:

_____

_____

CERTIFICATE OF INCORPORATION

OF

NEWCO, INC.*

The undersigned, for the purpose of organizing a corporation (the "Corporation") pursuant to the provisions of the General Corporation Law of the State of Delaware ("General Corporation Law"), does make and file this Certificate of Incorporation and does hereby certify as follows:

NEWCO, INC. (the "Corporation"), a corporation organized and existing under and by virtue of the General Corporation Law of the State of Delaware, does hereby certify as follows:

I. That its Certificate of Incorporation, filed with the Secretary of State of Delaware on _____,199_, is hereby amended and restated in its entirety to read as follows:

FIRST: Name: The name of the corporation is Newco, Inc.

SECOND: Registered Office: The registered office of the Corporation is to be located at 1209 Orange Street, City of Wilmington, County of New Castle, State of Delaware 19801. The name of its registered agent is The Corporation Trust Company, whose address is Corporation Trust Center, 1209 Orange Street, Wilmington, Delaware 19801.

The name of its registered agent is the Corporation Service Company, whose address is Corporation Service Company, 1013 Center Road, Wilmington,

---

* Useful treatises on organizing Delaware corporations include Halloran, Benton, Gunderson, Kearney & de Calvo, Venture Capital and Public Offering Negotiation (2d ed.) (hereinafter Halloran) and Balotti & Finkelstein, The Delaware Law of Corporations and Business Organizations (2d ed.) (hereinafter Balotti).

County of New Castle, Delaware 19805; [OR] The Prentice-Hall Corporation System, Inc. (PH), 32 Loockerman Square, Suite L-100, Dover, Delaware, 19901, County of Kent.

Rider 1 (not supplied)

THIRD: Purposes: The purpose of the Corporation is to engage in any lawful act or activity for which corporations may be organized under the General Corporation Law of the State of Delaware.

FOURTH. The total number of shares of stock the Corporation shall have authority to issue is (i) _,000,000 shares of Common Stock, $.01 par value per share ("Common Stock"), and (ii) _,000,000 shares of Preferred Stock, $.01 par value per share ("Preferred Stock").

The following is a statement of the designations and the powers, privileges and rights, and the qualifications, limitations or restrictions in respect of each class of capital stock of the Corporation.

A.   COMMON STOCK.

1.   General. The voting, dividend and liquidation rights of the holders of the Common Stock are subject to and qualified by the rights of the holders of the Preferred Stock of any series as may be designated by the Board of Directors upon any issuance of the Preferred Stock of any series.

2.   Voting. The holders of Common Stock are entitled to one vote for each share held at all meetings of stockholders (and written actions in lieu of meetings).

3.   Dividends. Dividends shall be declared and paid on the Common Stock from funds lawfully available therefor as and when determined by the Board of Directors and subject to any preferential dividend rights of any then outstanding Preferred Stock.

4.   Liquidation. Upon the dissolution or liquidation of the Corporation, whether voluntary or involuntary, all of the assets of the Corporation available for distribution to its stockholders shall be distributed ratably among the holders of the Preferred Stock, if any, and of the Common Stock, subject to any preferential rights of any then outstanding Preferred Stock.

B.   PREFERRED STOCK.

Preferred Stock may be issued from time to time in one or more series, each of such series to have such terms as stated or expressed in this Section B of Article FOURTH and/or in the resolution or resolutions providing for the issue of such series adopted by the Board of Directors of the Corporation as hereinafter provided. Any shares of Preferred Stock which may be redeemed, purchased or acquired by the Corporation may be reissued except as otherwise provided by law. Different series of Preferred Stock shall not be construed to constitute different classes of shares for the purposes of voting by classes unless expressly provided.

Authority is hereby granted to the Board of Directors from time to time to issue the Preferred Stock in one or more series, and in connection with the creation of any such series, by resolution or resolutions providing for the issuance of the shares thereof, to determine and fix such voting powers, full or limited, or no voting powers, and such designations, preferences, powers and relative participating, optional or other special rights and qualifications, limitations, or restrictions thereof, including without limitation dividend rights, conversion rights, redemption privileges and liquidation preferences, as shall be stated and expressed in such votes, all to the full extent now or hereafter permitted by the General Corporation Law. Without limiting the generality of the foregoing, the resolutions providing for issuance of any series of Preferred Stock may provide that such series shall be superior or rank equally or be junior to the Preferred Stock of any other series to the extent permitted by law. Except as provided in this Article FOURTH, no vote of the holders of the Preferred Stock or Common Stock shall be prerequisite to the issuance of any shares of any series of Preferred Stock authorized by and complying with the conditions of the Certificate of Incorporation, the right to enjoy such vote being expressly waived by all present and future holders of the capital stock of the Corporation. The resolutions providing for issuance of any series of Preferred Stock may provide that such resolutions may be amended by subsequent resolutions adopted in the same manner as the preceding resolutions. Such resolutions shall be effective upon adoption, without the necessity of any filing, with the Secretary of State of Delaware or otherwise.

C.   CUMULATIVE VOTING. At each election of directors, each shareholder entitled to vote at such election has the right: (a) to vote the number of voting shares owned by him for as many persons as there are directors to be elected (and for whose election such shareholder has a right to vote); or (b) to cumulate his votes by giving one nominee as many votes as the number of such directors multiplied by the number of his shares shall equal, or by distributing such votes on the same principle among any number of such nominees.

A shareholder who intends to cumulate his votes shall give written notice of such intention to the secretary of the Corporation on or before the day preceding the election at which such shareholder intends to cumulate his votes. All shareholders shall be given notice if any shareholder gives such notice and may thereupon cumulate their votes.

D.   <u>RESTRICTIONS ON TRANSFER</u>.   The following restrictions are imposed upon the transfer of shares of the capital stock of the Corporation:

The Corporation shall have the right to purchase, or to direct the transfer of, the shares of its capital stock in the events and subject to the conditions and at a price fixed as provided below. Each holder of shares of such capital stock holds his shares subject to this right and by accepting the same upon original issuance or subsequent transfer thereof, the holder agrees for himself, his legal representatives and assigns as follows:

In the event of any change in the ownership of any share or shares of such capital stock (made or proposed) or in the right to vote thereon (whether by the holder's act or by death, legal disability, operation of law, legal processes, order of court, or otherwise, except by ordinary proxies or powers of attorney), the Corporation has the right to purchase all or any part of such shares or to require the same to be sold to a purchaser or purchasers designated by the Corporation, or to follow each such method in part, at a price per share equal to the fair value thereof at the close of business on the last business day next preceding such event as determined by mutual agreement or, failing such agreement, by arbitration as provided below. Fair value, for this purpose, shall be determined as if the Corporation was being sold to an unaffiliated third party as an entry, with no discount applied to the shares by reason of illiquidity or minority position.

In any such event the owner of the share or shares concerned therein (being, for the purposes of these provisions, all persons having any actual or inchoate property interest therein) shall give notice thereof in detail satisfactory to the Corporation. Within ten (10) days after receipt of said owner's notice, the Corporation shall elect whether or not to exercise its said rights in respect to said shares and, if it elects to exercise them, shall give notice of its election.

Failing agreement between the owner and the Corporation as to the price per share to be paid, such price shall be the fair value of such shares as determined by three (3) arbitrators, one designated within five (5) days after the termination of said ten (10) day period by the registered holder of said share or shares or his legal representatives, one within said period of five (5) days by the Corporation, and the third within five (5) days after said appointment last occurring by the two (2) so chosen. Successor arbitrators, if any shall be required, shall be appointed, within reasonable time, as nearly as may be in the manner provided as to the related original appointment. No appointment shall be deemed as having been accomplished unless such arbitrator shall have accepted in writing his appointment as such within the time limited for his appointment. Notice of each appointment of an arbitrator shall be given promptly to the other parties in interest. Said arbitrators shall proceed promptly to determine said fair value. The determination of the fair value of said share or shares by agreement of any two (2) of the arbitrators shall be conclusive upon all parties interested in such shares. Forthwith upon such determination the arbitrators shall mail or deliver notice of such determination to the owner (as above defined) and to the Corporation. The reasonable fees and expenses of the arbitrators shall be paid by the Corporation.

Within ten (10) days after agreement upon said price or mailing of notice of determination of said price by the arbitrators as provided above (whichever shall last occur), the shares specified therein for purchase shall be transferred to the Corporation or to the purchaser or purchasers designated therein or in part to each as indicated in such notice of election against payment of said price at the principal office of the Corporation.

If in any of the said events, notice therefor having been given as provided above, the Corporation elects in respect of any such shares or any part thereof not to exercise its said rights, or fails to exercise them or to give notice or make payment, all as provided above, or waives said rights by vote or in authorized writing, then such contemplated transfer or such change may become effective as to those shares with respect to which the Corporation elects not to exercise its rights or fails to exercise them or to give notice or to make payment, if consummated within thirty (30) days after such election, failure or waiver by the Corporation, or within such longer period as the Corporation may authorize.

If the owner's notice in respect of any of such shares of capital stock is not received by the Corporation as provided above, or if the owner fails to comply with these provisions in respect of any such shares in any other regard, the Corporation, at its option and in addition to its other remedies, may suspend the rights to vote or to receive dividends on said shares, or may refuse to register on its books any transfer of said shares or otherwise to recognize any transfer or change in the ownership thereof or in the right to vote thereon, one or more, until these provisions are complied with to the satisfaction of the Corporation; and if the required owner's notice is not received by the Corporation after written demand by the Corporation, it may also or independently proceed as though a proper owner's notice had been received at the expiration of ten days after mailing such demand, and, if it exercises its rights with respect to said shares or any of them, the shares specified shall be transferred, and/or deemed transferred, accordingly.

In respect of these provisions, the Corporation may act by its Board of Directors, not including the vote of any director personally interested in the transfer. Any notice or demand under said provisions shall be deemed to have been sufficiently given if in writing, delivered by hand or addressed by mail postpaid, to the Corporation at its principal office or to the owner (as above defined) or to the holder registered on the books of the Corporation (or his legal representative) of the share or shares in question at the address stated in his notice or at his address appearing on the books of the Corporation. Nothing herein contained shall prevent the pledging of shares if there is neither a transfer of the legal title thereto nor a transfer on the books of the Corporation into the name of the pledgee. But no pledgee or person claiming thereunder shall be entitled to make or cause to be made any transfer of pledged shares by sale thereof or otherwise (including in this prohibition transfers on the books of the Corporation into the name of the pledgee) except upon compliance herewith, and any such pledge shall be subject to those conditions and restrictions.

FIFTH: Indemnity: The Corporation shall, to the fullest extent legally permissible, indemnify (fully or, if not possible, partially) each of its directors and officers, and persons who serve at its request as directors or officers of another organization in which it owns shares or of which it is a creditor, against all liabilities (including expenses) imposed upon or reasonably incurred by him or her in connection with any action, suit or other proceeding, civil or criminal (including investigations, audits, the activities of, or service upon special committees of the board) in which he or she may be involved or with which he or she may be threatened, while in office or thereafter, by reason of his acts or omissions as such director or officer, unless in any proceeding he or she shall be finally adjudged not to have acted in good faith in the reasonable belief that his action was in the best interest of the Corporation; provided, however, that such indemnification shall not cover liabilities in connection with any matter which shall be disposed of through a compromise payment by such director or officer, pursuant to a consent decree or otherwise, unless such compromise shall be approved as in the best interest of the Corporation, after notice that it involved such indemnification, (a) by a vote of the directors in which no interested director participates, or (b) by a vote or the written approval of the holders of a majority of the outstanding stock at the time having the right to vote for directors, not counting as outstanding any stock owned by any interested director or officer. Such indemnification may include payment by the Corporation of expenses incurred in defending a civil or criminal action or proceeding in advance of the final disposition of such action or proceeding, upon receipt of an undertaking by the person indemnified to repay such payment if he or she shall be adjudicated to be not entitled to indemnification under these provisions. The rights of indemnification hereby provided shall not be exclusive of or affect other rights to which any director or officer may be entitled. As used in this paragraph, the terms "director" and "officer" include their respective heirs, executors and administrators, and an "interested" director or officer is one against whom as such the proceedings in question or another proceeding on the same or similar grounds is then pending.

Indemnification of employees and other agents of the Corporation (including persons who serve at its request as employees or other agents of another organization in which it owns shares or of which it is a creditor) may be provided by the Corporation to whatever extent shall be authorized by the directors before or after the occurrence of any event as to or in consequence of which indemnification may be sought. Any indemnification to which a person is entitled under these provisions may be provided although the person to be indemnified is no longer a director, officer, employee or agent of the Corporation or of such other organization. It is the intent of these provisions to indemnify director and officers to the fullest extent not specifically prohibited by law, including indemnification against claims brought derivatively, in the name of the Corporation, and that such directors and officers need not exhaust any other remedies.

SIXTH: Meetings: Elections: Meetings of the stockholders may be held within or without the State of Delaware, as the Bylaws may provide. Subject to the provisions of any law or regulation, the books of the Corporation may be kept outside the State of Delaware at such place or places as may be designated from time to time by the Board of Directors or in the Bylaws of the Corporation. The election of directors need not be by written ballot unless the Bylaws so provide.

SEVENTH: Bylaws: The board of directors of the Corporation is authorized and empowered from time to time in its discretion to make, alter, amend or repeal Bylaws of the Corporation, except as such power may be restricted or limited by the General Corporation Law.

EIGHTH: Compromise or Arrangement: Whenever a compromise or arrangement is proposed between the Corporation and its creditors or any class of them and/or between the Corporation and its stockholders or any class of them, any court of equitable jurisdiction within the State of Delaware may, on the application in a summary way of the Corporation or of any creditor or stockholder thereof, or on the application of any receiver or receivers appointed for the Corporation under the provision of § 291 of the General Corporation Law, or on the application of trustees in dissolution or of any receiver or receivers appointed for the Corporation under § 279 of the General Corporation Law, order a meeting of the creditors or class of creditors, and/or of the stockholders or class of stockholders of the Corporation, as the case may be, to be summoned in such manner as the said court directs. If a majority in number representing three-fourths in value of the creditors or class of creditors, and/or of the stockholders or class of stockholders of the Corporation, as the case may be, agree to any compromise or arrangement and to any reorganization of the Corporation as a consequence of such compromise or arrangement, the said compromise or arrangement and the said reorganization shall, if sanctioned by the court to which said application has been made, be binding on all the creditors or class of creditors, and/or on all the stockholders or class of stockholders of the Corporation, as the case may be, and also on the Corporation.

NINTH: Exculpation: No director shall be personally liable to the Corporation or its stockholders for monetary damages for any breach of fiduciary duty by such director as a director. Notwithstanding the foregoing sentence, a director shall be liable to the extent provided by applicable law (i) for any breach of the director's Duty of Loyalty (as herein defined) to the Corporation or its stockholders, (ii) for acts or omissions not in good faith or which involve intentional misconduct or a knowing violation of law, (iii) under § 174 of the General Corporation Law, or (iv) for any transaction from which the director derived an improper personal benefit. For purposes of this provision, Duty of Loyalty means, and only means, the duty not to profit personally at the expense of the Corporation and does not include conduct, whether deemed violation of fiduciary duty or otherwise, which does not involve personal monetary profit.

TENTH: Reservation of Amendment Power: Subject to the limitations set forth herein, the Corporation reserves the right to amend, alter, change or repeal any provision contained in this Certificate of Incorporation, in the manner now or hereafter prescribed by law, and all rights and powers conferred herein on stockholders, directors and officers are subject to this reserved power.

ELEVENTH: Management: Except as otherwise required by law, by the Certificate of Incorporation or by the Bylaws of the Corporation, as from time to time amended, the business of the Corporation shall be managed by its board of directors, which shall have and may exercise all the powers of the Corporation. The board of directors of the Corporation is hereby specifically authorized and empowered from time to time in its discretion to determine the extent, if any, to which and the time and place at which, and the conditions under which any stockholder of the Corporation may examine books and records of the Corporation, other than the books and records now or hereafter required by statute to be kept open for inspection of stockholders of the Corporation.

TWELFTH: Liquidation: Any vote or votes authorizing liquidation of the Corporation or proceedings for its dissolution may provide, subject to the rights of creditors and rights expressly provided for particular classes or series of stock, for the distribution pro rata among the stockholders of the Corporation of the assets of the Corporation, wholly or in part in kind, whether such assets be in cash or other property, and may authorize the board of directors of the Corporation to determine the value of the different assets of the Corporation for the purpose of such liquidation and may authorize the board of directors of the Corporation to divide such assets or any part thereof among the stockholders of the Corporation, in such manner that every stockholder will receive a proportionate amount in value (determined as aforesaid) of cash or property of the Corporation upon such liquidation or dissolution even though each stockholder may not receive a strictly proportionate part of each such asset.

THIRTEENTH: Purchase of Shares: The Corporation may purchase directly or indirectly its own shares to the extent the money or other property paid or the indebtedness issued therefore does not (i) render the Corporation unable to pay its debts as they become due in the usual course of business or (ii) exceed the surplus of the Corporation, as defined in the General Corporation Law. Notwithstanding the limitations contained in the preceding sentence, the Corporation may purchase any of its own shares for the following purposes, provided that the net assets of the Corporation, as defined in the General Corporation Law, are not less than the amount of money or other property paid or the indebtedness issued therefor: (i) to eliminate fractional shares; (ii) to collect or compromise indebtedness owed by or to the Corporation; (iii) to pay dissenting shareholders entitled to payment for their shares under the General Corporation Law; and (iv) to effect the purchase or redemption of redeemable shares in accordance with the General Corporation Law.

FOURTEENTH: Section 203 Opt Out

The Corporation hereby elects not to be governed by § 203 of the General Corporation Law of the State of Delaware as from time to time in effect or any successor provision thereto.

Comment: *See Treatise § 4.15 - this article addresses a provision of the G.C.L. that limits transactions with interested directors.*

FIFTEENTH: The name and address of the Incorporator is:

[Name]
[Address
[City] [State] [Zip Code]

The name and mailing address of each person who is to serve as a director of the Corporation is as follows, each to serve and hold office until the earliest of (a) the first annual meeting of stockholders, (b) his or her successor is elected and qualified, or (c) his or her death, resignation or removal from office.

Name   Mailing Address

[To be inserted]   [To be inserted]

The above [Amended and Restated] Certificate of Incorporation, herein certified, has been duly adopted in accordance with the provisions of Sections 228, 242 and 245 of the General Corporation Law.

IN WITNESS WHEREOF, the undersigned has hereunto set <his/her> hand this ___ day of [month], 199_.

                              INCORPORATOR:

                              _____

                              [Name]

IN WITNESS WHEREOF, the Corporation has caused this Certificate to be executed by its President and attested to by its Secretary this _____ day of [month], 199_.

Newco Inc.

_____ [Name], President

ATTEST:

CERTIFICATE OF DESIGNATION OF SERIES

AND DETERMINATION OF RIGHTS AND PREFERENCES

OF

CUMULATIVE CONVERTIBLE PREFERRED STOCK, SERIES A

OF

NEWCO, INC.

Newco, Inc., a Delaware corporation (the "Company"), acting pursuant to Section 151 of the General Company Law of Delaware, does hereby submit the following Certificate of Designation of Series and Determination of Rights and Preferences of its Convertible Preferred Stock, Series A.

FIRST: The name of the Company is Newco, Inc.

SECOND: By unanimous consent of the Board of Directors of the Company dated [month], 199_, the following resolutions were duly adopted:

WHEREAS the Certificate of Incorporation of the Company authorizes Preferred Stock consisting of _____ shares, par value $.01 per share, issuable from time to time in one or more series; and

WHEREAS the Board of Directors of the Company is authorized, subject to limitations prescribed by law and by the provisions of Article FOURTH of the Company's Certificate of Incorporation, as amended, to establish and fix the number of shares to be included in any series of Preferred Stock and the designation, rights, preferences, powers, restrictions and limitations of the shares of such series; and

WHEREAS it is the desire of the Board of Directors to establish and fix the number of shares to be included in a new series of Preferred Stock and the designation, rights, preferences and limitations of the shares of such new series;

NOW, THEREFORE, BE IT RESOLVED that pursuant to Article FOURTH of the Company's Certificate of Incorporation, as amended, there is hereby established a new series of _____ shares of cumulative convertible preferred Stock of the Company (the "Series A Preferred Stock") to have the designation, rights, preferences, powers, restrictions and limitations set forth in a supplement of Article FOURTH as follows:

1.   Dividends.

(a)   The holders of the Series A Preferred Stock shall be entitled to receive, out of funds legally available therefor, cumulative dividends at the rate of $____ (subject to appropriate adjustments in the event of any stock dividend, stock split, combination or other similar recapitalization affecting such shares) per share per annum, and no more, payable in preference and priority to any payment of any cash dividend on Common Stock or any other shares of capital stock of the Company other than the Series A Preferred Stock or other class or series of stock ranking on a par with, or senior to the Series A Preferred Stock in respect of dividends (such Common Stock and other inferior stock being collectively referred to as "Junior Stock"), when and as declared by the Board of Directors of the Company.

> Comment: *Once a dividend is declared, it is owed. Accrued dividends, by the terms of this Agreement, see § 4(a), entitle the holder to preference upon liquidation but disappear upon conversion. Alternatively, the certificate may specify payment whenever payment is appropriate. The language is as follows:*

Such dividends shall accrue with respect to each share of Series A Preferred Stock from the date on which such share is issued and outstanding and thereafter shall be deemed to accrue from day to day whether or not earned or declared and whether or not there exists profits, surplus or other funds legally available for the payment of dividends, and shall be cumulative so that if such dividends on the Series A Preferred Stock shall not have been paid, or declared and set apart for payment, the deficiency shall be fully paid or declared and set apart for payment before any dividend shall be paid or declared or set apart for any Junior Stock and before any purchase or acquisition of any Junior Stock is made by the Company, except the repurchase of Junior Stock from employees of the Company upon termination of employment. At the earlier of: (i) the redemption of the Series A Preferred Stock; (ii) the filing of a registration statement in respect of an underwritten public offering of the type described in Section 5(a); or (iii) the liquidation, sale or merger of the Company, any accrued but undeclared dividends shall be paid to the holders of record of outstanding shares of Series A Preferred Stock. No accumulation of dividends on the Series A Preferred Stock shall bear interest.

> Comment: *In early stage issuers, preferred dividends are occasionally specified as non-cumulative because there is no expectation dividends will actually be paid. However, the most common practice is to accumulate dividends, even if they are not expected to be paid, because the cash investors expect to be preferred vis a vis the junior holders if and as the issuer is sold at a price which makes conversion unattractive.*

> Comment: *If there is to be a PIK (payment in kind) option, the language is as follows:*

At the election of the Company, each dividend may be paid either in additional shares of Series A Preferred Stock or in cash until July 1, 199_ and payable only in cash from thereafter until July 1, 200_. Dividends paid in additional shares of Series A Preferred Stock shall be paid in full shares only,, with a cash payment (based on an assumed value of $_____ per share) equal to the value of any fractional shares. Each dividend paid in cash shall be mailed to the holders of record of the Series A Preferred Stock as their names and addresses appear on the share register of the Company or at the office of the transfer agent on the corresponding dividend payment date. Holders of Series A Preferred Stock will receive written notification from the Company or the transfer agent if a dividend is paid in kind, which notification will specify the number of shares of Series A Preferred Stock paid as a dividend and the recipient's aggregate holdings of Series A Preferred Stock as of that dividend payment date and after giving effect to the dividend.

  2. Liquidation, Dissolution or Winding Up.

    (a) In the event of any voluntary or involuntary liquidation, dissolution or winding up of the Company, the holders of shares of Series A Preferred Stock then outstanding shall be entitled to be paid out of the assets of the Company available for distribution to its stockholders, after and subject to the payment in full of all amounts required to be distributed to the holders of any other class or series of stock of the Company ranking on liquidation prior and in preference to the Series A Preferred Stock (collectively referred to as "Senior Preferred Stock"), but before any payment shall be made to the holders of Common Stock or any other class or series of stock ranking on liquidation junior to the Series A Preferred Stock (such Common Stock and other stock being collectively referred to as "Junior Stock") by reason of their ownership thereof, an amount equal to $\$\_\_$ per share of Series A Preferred Stock plus any accrued but unpaid dividends (whether or not declared). If upon any such liquidation, dissolution or winding up of the Company the remaining assets of the Company available for distribution to its stockholders shall be insufficient to pay the holders of shares of Series A Preferred Stock the full amount to which they shall be entitled, the holders of shares of Series A Preferred Stock and any class or series of stock (the "Preferred Stock") ranking on liquidation on a parity with the Series A Preferred Stock shall share ratably in any distribution of the remaining assets and funds of the Company in proportion to the respective amounts which would otherwise be payable in respect of the shares held by them upon such distribution if all amounts payable on or with respect to such shares were paid in full.

    (b) After the payment of all preferential amounts required to be paid to the holders of Senior Preferred Stock, upon the dissolution, liquidation or winding up of the Company, all of the remaining assets and funds of the Company available for distribution to its stockholders shall be distributed ratably among the holders of the Series A Preferred Stock, such other series of Preferred Stock as are constituted as similarly participating and the Common Stock, with each share of Series A Preferred Stock being deemed, for such purpose, to be equal to the number of shares of Common Stock, including fractions of a share, into which such share of Series A

Preferred Stock is convertible immediately prior to the close of business on the business day fixed for such distribution.

> Comment: *This provision allows the preferred to participate after payment of the preferred dividend (thus a "Participating Preferred") and is, therefore, a strong pro-preferred provision. See 1 Halloran 7-13.*

(c)　　The merger or consolidation of the Company into or with another corporation which results in the exchange of outstanding shares of the Company for securities or other consideration issued or paid or caused to be issued or paid by such other corporation or an affiliate thereof (except if such merger or consolidation does not result in the transfer of more than 50% of the voting securities of the Company), or the sale of all or substantially all the assets of the Company, shall be deemed to be a liquidation, dissolution or winding up of the Company for purposes of this Section, unless the holders of sixty-six and two-thirds percent (66-2/3%) of the Series A Preferred Stock then outstanding vote otherwise.　The amount deemed distributed to the holders of Series A Preferred Stock upon any such merger or consolidation shall be the cash or the value of the property, rights and/or securities distributed to such holders by the acquiring person, firm or other entity.　The value of such property, rights or other securities shall be determined in good faith by the Board of Directors of the Company.

> Comment: *This is a strong pro-preferred instrument; See 1 Halloran 7-18. Thus, assume the corporation merges into Newco for Newco stock, notes and cash which the board values at $1,000,000 in toto. The Series A Preferred is paid its liquidation preference and accrued dividends first - say $500,000 - then shares pari passu (say 50/50) with the common stock in the overage, meaning the preferred takes $750,000, vs. $500,000 (ignoring accrued dividends) were it to convert (figuring accrued dividends).*

3.　　Voting.

(a)　　Each holder of outstanding shares of Series A Preferred Stock shall be entitled to the number of votes equal to the number of whole shares of Common Stock into which the shares of Series A Preferred Stock held by such holder are convertible (as adjusted from time to time pursuant to Section 4 hereof), at each meeting of stockholders of the Company (and written actions of stockholders in lieu of meetings) with respect to any and all matters presented to the stockholders of the Company for their action or consideration.　So long as the holders of Series A Preferred Stock hold forty percent (40%) or more of the aggregate voting rights of the Series A Preferred

Stock and Common Stock, the holders of the Series A Preferred Stock shall be entitled to elect that number of directors that is the lowest number that constitutes a majority of the members of the Board of Directors, and the holders of the Common Stock shall be entitled to elect the remaining members of the Board of Directors. So long as the holders of Series A Preferred Stock hold twenty percent (20%) or more, but less than forty percent (40%) of the aggregate voting rights of the Series A Preferred Stock and Common Stock, the holders of the Series A Preferred Stock shall have the right to elect that number of directors that is one person lower than the lowest number that constitutes a majority of the members of the Board of Directors, and the remaining directors shall be elected by the holders of the Series A Preferred Stock and Common Stock voting together. Those Directors elected by the holders of Series A Preferred Stock shall be referred to as "Investor Directors." [At least one of the Investor Directors shall be an "outside director," as designated by name in the Shareholders Agreement.] Except as provided by law, by the provisions of Subsection 3(b) or 3(c) below or by the provisions establishing any other series of Preferred Stock, holders of Series A Preferred Stock and of any other outstanding series of Preferred Stock shall vote together with the holders of Common Stock as a single class.

> Comment: *Given a preferred stock designed to pay dividends currently, a default in payment often shifts voting power entirely to the preferred. See Treatise § 13.4.*

(b)   Protective Provisions. Without the affirmative vote or consent of holders of at least a majority of the Series A Preferred Stock at the time outstanding, voting separately as a class, the corporation shall not:

(i)   Authorize or issue any (i) additional Series A Preferred Stock or (ii) shares of stock having priority over Series A Preferred Stock or ranking on a parity therewith as to the payment of dividends or as to the payment or distribution of assets upon the liquidation or dissolution, voluntary or involuntary, of the corporation; or

(ii)   Declare or pay any dividend or make any other distribution on any shares of capital stock of the corporation at any time created and issued ranking junior to Series A Preferred Stock with respect to the right to receive dividends and the right to the distribution of assets upon liquidation, dissolution or winding up of the corporation (hereinafter called "Junior Stock"), other than dividends or distributions payable solely in shares of Junior Stock, or purchase, redeem or otherwise acquire for any consideration (other than in exchange for or out of the net cash proceeds of the contemporaneous issue or sale of other shares of Junior Stock), or set aside as a sinking fund or other fund for the redemption or repurchase of any shares of

Junior Stock or any warrants, rights or options to purchase shares of Junior Stock, except as specifically permitted by the terms of the Stock Purchase Agreement;

(iii)   Amend the articles of incorporation of the corporation so as to adversely affect any of the rights, preferences or privileges of the holders of Series A Preferred Stock; or

(iv)   Sell, lease, license or otherwise dispose of all or substantially all of its assets, or consolidate with or merge into any other corporation or entity, or permit any other corporation or entity to consolidate or merge into it, except that any subsidiary of the corporation may merge into another subsidiary or into the corporation.

(c)   Event of Default. Upon the occurrence of an Event of Default, as that term is defined in the Stock Purchase Agreement, the holders of Series A Preferred Stock shall be entitled to elect that number of directors that is the lowest number that constitutes a majority of the members of the Board of Directors, and the holders of Common Stock shall be entitled to elect the remaining members of the Board of Directors. The right of the holders of Series A Preferred Stock to vote as provided in this subsection 3(c) shall cease upon the curing of the Event of Default which gave rise to such right and the curing of all Events of Default occurring after the Event of Default which gave rise to such right.

(d)   Special Election Procedures. At any time after the right to elect a majority of the members of the Board of Directors shall have become vested in the holders of Series A Preferred Stock as provided in subsection 3(c) or subsection 3(a), the secretary of the corporation may, and upon the request of the record holders of at least twenty percent (20%) of the outstanding shares of Series A Preferred Stock addressed to the secretary at the principal executive office of the corporation shall call a meeting for the election of directors, to be held at the place and upon the notice provided in the bylaws of the corporation for the holding of a regular meeting. If such meeting shall not be so called within ten (10) days after personal service of the request, or within fifteen (15) days after mailing of the same by registered mail within the United States of America, then a person designated by the record holders of at least twenty percent (20%) of the outstanding shares of Series A Preferred Stock may call such meeting at the place and upon the notice above provided and for that purpose shall have the right, during regular business hours, to examine and to make copies of extracts of the stock records of the corporation. At any meeting so called or at any regular meeting held while the holders of the Series A Preferred Stock have the right to elect a majority of the members of the Board of Directors as provided in subsection 3(c) or subsection 3(a), the holders of a majority of the then-outstanding shares of Series A Preferred Stock, present in person or by proxy, shall be sufficient to constitute a quorum for the election of directors as herein provided. The terms of office of all persons who are directors of the corporation at the time of such meeting shall terminate upon the election at such meeting by the holders of the Series A Preferred Stock of the number of directors they are entitled to elect and the persons so elected as directors by the holders of Series A Preferred Stock, together with such persons, if any, as may be elected directors by the holders of Common Stock, shall constitute the duly elected directors of the corporation. In the event the holders of Common Stock fail to elect any of the directors which they are entitled to elect at such meeting, additional directors may be appointed by the directors elected by the holders of Series A Preferred Stock. If, during any interval between regular meetings of shareholders while the holders of Series A Preferred Stock are entitled to elect a majority of the Board of Directors after the initial election by such holders has been made, the number of directors who have been elected by the holders of Series A Preferred Stock or the holders of Common Stock, as the case may be, shall, by reason of resignation, death or removal, be less than the total number of directors subject to election by all such holders, any vacancy in directors elected by the holders of Common Stock shall be filled by a majority vote of the remaining directors then in office who were elected by the holders of Common Stock or succeeded a director so elected, although such majority be less than a quorum, and any vacancy in the directors elected by the holders of Series A Preferred Stock shall be filled by a majority of the remaining directors then in office who were elected by the holders of Series A Preferred Stock or succeeded a director so elected, although such majority may be less than a quorum.

Whenever the voting rights of Series A Preferred Stock shall cease as provided in subsection 3(c), the Board of Directors shall call a meeting of shareholders at which all directors will be elected as provided in subsection 3(a) above and the term of office of all persons who are then directors of the corporation shall terminate immediately upon the election of their successors.

Comment: *For a more elaborate version of "change of control", see App. A-10 to A-15.*

4.   Optional Conversion.

The holders of the Series A Preferred Stock shall have conversion rights as follows (the "Conversion Rights"):

(a)   Right to Convert. Each share of Series A Preferred Stock shall be convertible, at the option of the holder thereof, at any time and from time to time, into such number of fully paid and nonassessable shares of Common Stock as is determined by dividing ten dollars ($10.00) by the Conversion Price (as defined below) in effect at the time of conversion. The Conversion Price at which shares of Common Stock shall be deliverable upon conversion of Series A Preferred Stock without the payment of additional consideration by the holder thereof (the "Conversion Price") shall initially be ten dollars ($10.00). Such initial Conversion Price, and the rate at which shares of Series A Preferred Stock may be converted into shares of Common Stock, shall be subject to adjustment as provided below.

> <u>Comment</u>: *Note that, under this provision, preferred stockholders lose accrued but unpaid dividends upon conversion.*

> <u>Comment</u>: *To start with, each share of Preferred converts into one share of common under the above provision. The base amount (ten dollars, in the above case) is usually the liquidation preference of the preferred and in fact what the investors paid per preferred share. On occasion, the holders of a given Series shall have the right to payment of accrued but unpaid dividends on the eve of conversion. See Treatise §§ 13.4, 13.5.*

In the event of a liquidation of the Company, the Conversion Rights shall terminate at the close of business on the first full day preceding the date fixed for the payment of any amounts distributable on liquidation to the holders of Series A Preferred Stock.

(b)   Fractional Shares. No fractional shares of Common Stock shall be issued upon conversion of the Series A Preferred Stock. In lieu of fractional shares, the Company shall pay cash equal to such fraction multiplied by the then effective Conversion Price.

(c)   Mechanics of Conversion.

(i)   In order to convert shares of Series A Preferred Stock into shares of Common Stock, the holder shall surrender the certificate or certificates for such shares of Series A Preferred Stock at the office of the transfer agent (or at the principal office of the Company if the Company serves as its own transfer agent), together with written notice that such holder elects to convert all or any number of the shares represented by such certificate or certificates. Such notice shall state such holder's name or the names of the nominees to which such holder wishes the certificate or certificates for shares of Common Stock to be issued. If required by the Company, certificates surrendered for conversion shall be endorsed or accompanied by a written instrument or instruments of transfer, in form satisfactory to the Company, duly executed by the registered holder or his or its attorney duly authorized in writing. The date of receipt of such certificates and notice by the transfer agent or the Company shall be the conversion date ("Conversion Date"). The Company shall, as soon as practicable after the Conversion Date, issue and deliver at such office to such holder, or to his nominees, a certificate or certificates for the number of shares of Common Stock to which such holder shall be entitled, together with cash in lieu of any fraction of a share.

(ii)   The Company shall at all times during which the Series A Preferred Stock shall be outstanding, reserve and keep available out of its authorized but unissued stock, for the purpose of effecting the conversion of the Series A Preferred Stock, such number of its duly authorized shares of Common Stock as shall from time to time be sufficient to effect the conversion of all outstanding Series A Preferred Stock. Before taking any action which would cause an adjustment reducing the Conversion Price below the then par value of the shares of Common Stock issuable upon conversion of the Series A Preferred Stock, the Company will take any corporate action which may, in the opinion of its counsel, be necessary in order that the Company may validly and legally issue fully paid and nonassessable shares of Common Stock at such adjusted Conversion Price.

(iii)   Upon any such conversion, no adjustment to the Conversion Price shall be made for any accrued and unpaid dividends on the Series A Preferred Stock surrendered for conversion or on the Common Stock delivered upon conversion; the holder, by converting, waives his right to such accrued but unpaid dividends.

> Comment: *If the idea is that accrued dividends are part of the holder's outcome in any event, then the cash element converts into common stock by dividing the Conversion Price into ten dollars plus accrued but unpaid dividends.*

(iv)   All shares of Series A Preferred Stock, which shall have been surrendered for conversion as herein provided shall no longer be deemed to be outstanding and all rights with respect to such shares, including the rights, if any, to receive dividends, and notices and to vote, shall immediately cease and terminate on the Conversion Date, except only the right of the holders thereof to receive shares of Common Stock in exchange therefor.
Any shares of Series A Preferred Stock so converted shall be retired and cancelled and shall not be reissued, and the Company may from time to time take such appropriate action as may be necessary to reduce the number of shares of authorized Series A Preferred Stock accordingly.

Comment: *As earlier indicated, some instruments contemplate a cash payment of accrued dividends upon conversion.*

(v) If the conversion is in connection with an underwritten offer of securities registered pursuant to the Securities Act of 1933, as amended, the conversion may at the option of any holder tendering Series A Preferred Stock for conversion, be conditioned upon the closing with the underwriter of the sale of securities pursuant to such offering, in which event the person(s) entitled to receive the Common Stock issuable upon such conversion of the Series A Preferred Stock shall not be deemed to have converted such Series A Preferred Stock until immediately prior to the closing of the sale of securities.

(d) Adjustments to Conversion Price for Diluting Issues.

(i) Special Definitions. For purposes of this Subsection 4(d), the following definitions shall apply:

(A) "Option" shall mean rights, options or warrants to subscribe for, purchase or otherwise acquire Common Stock or Convertible Securities, excluding rights or options granted to employees, directors or consultants of the Company pursuant to an option plan adopted by the Board of Directors to acquire up to that number of shares of Common Stock as is equal to fifteen percent (15%) of the Common Stock outstanding (provided that, for purposes of this Subsection 4(d)(i)(A), all shares of Common Stock issuable upon (I) exercise of options granted or available for grant under plans approved by the Board of Directors, (II) conversion of shares of Preferred Stock, or (III) conversion of Preferred Stock issuable upon conversion or exchange of any Convertible Security, shall be deemed to be outstanding), minus the total number of Key Employee Shares (as defined below).

(B) "Original Issue Date" shall mean the date on which the first share of Series A Preferred Stock is first issued.

(C) "Convertible Securities" shall mean any evidences of indebtedness, shares or other securities directly or indirectly convertible into or exchangeable for Common Stock.

(D) "Additional Shares of Common Stock" shall mean all shares of Common Stock issued (or, pursuant to Subsection 4(d)(iii) below, deemed to be issued) by the Company after the Original Issue Date, other than Key Employee Shares (as defined below) and other than shares of Common Stock issued or issuable:

(I)   as   a   dividend   or distribution on Series A Preferred Stock;

(II)   by reason of a dividend, stock split, split-up or other distribution on shares of Common Stock excluded from the definition of Additional Shares of Common Stock by the foregoing clause (I);

(III)   upon   the   exercise   of options excluded from the definition of "Option" in Subsection 4(d)(i)(A);

(IV)   upon conversion of shares of Series A Preferred Stock; or

(E)   "Key Employee Shares" shall mean shares of Common Stock issued to directors or key employees of or consultants to the Company pursuant to a restricted stock plan or agreement approved by the Board of Directors, up to that number of shares of Common Stock as is equal to fifteen percent (15%) of the Common Stock outstanding (provided that, for purposes of this Subsection 4(d)(i)(E), all shares of Common Stock issuable upon (I) exercise of options granted or available for grant under plans approved by the Board of Directors, (II) conversion of shares of Preferred Stock, or (III) upon conversion of Preferred Stock issuable upon conversion or exchange of any Convertible Security, shall be deemed to be outstanding), minus the total number of shares subject to or issued pursuant to options excluded from the definition of "Option" in paragraph (A) above (subject to appropriate adjustment for any stock dividend, stock split, combination or similar recapitalization affecting such shares).

(F)   "Rights to Acquire Common Stock" (or "Rights") shall mean all rights issued by the Company to acquire common stock whatever by exercise of a warrant, option or similar call or conversion of any existing instruments, in either case for consideration fixed, in amount or by formula, as of the date of issuance.

(ii)   No Adjustment of Conversion Price. No adjustment in the number of shares of Common Stock into which the Series A

Preferred Stock is convertible shall be made, by adjustment in the applicable Conversion Price thereof: (a) unless the consideration per share (determined pursuant to Subsection 4(d)(v)) for an Additional Share of Common Stock issued or deemed to be issued by the Company is less than the applicable Conversion Price in effect on the date of, and immediately prior to, the issue of such Additional Shares, or (b) if prior to such issuance, the Company receives written notice from the holders of at least sixty six and two thirds percent (66-2/3%) of the then outstanding shares of Series A Preferred Stock agreeing that no such adjustment shall be made as the result of the issuance of Additional Shares of Common Stock.

(iii)   Issue of Securities Deemed Issue of Additional Shares of Common Stock. If the Company at any time or from time to time after the Original Issue Date shall issue any Options or Convertible Securities or other Rights to Acquire Common Stock, then the maximum number of shares of Common Stock (as set forth in the instrument relating thereto without regard to any provision contained therein for a subsequent adjustment of such number) issuable upon the exercise of such Options, Rights or, in the case of Convertible Securities, the conversion or exchange of such Convertible Securities, shall be deemed to be Additional Shares of Common Stock issued as of the time of such issue, provided that Additional Shares of Common Stock shall not be deemed to have been issued unless the consideration per share (determined pursuant to Subsection 4(d)(v) hereof) of such Additional Shares of Common Stock would be less than the applicable Conversion Price in effect on the date of and immediately prior to such issue, or such record date, as the case may be, and provided further that in any such case in which Additional Shares of Common Stock are deemed to be issued:

(A)   No further adjustment in the Conversion Price shall be made upon the subsequent issue of shares of Common Stock upon the exercise of such Rights or conversion or exchange of such Convertible Securities;

Comment: *Not covered are complex derivatives,... for example an option to acquire an option to acquire common stock.*

(B)   Upon the expiration or termination of any unexercised Option or Right, the Conversion Price shall not be readjusted, but the Additional Shares of Common Stock deemed issued as the result of the original issue of such Option or Right shall not be deemed issued for the purposes of any subsequent adjustment of the Conversion Price; and

(C)   In the event of any change in the number of shares of Common Stock issuable upon the exercise, conversion or exchange of any Option, Right or Convertible Security, including, but not limited to, a change resulting from the anti-dilution provisions thereof, the Conversion Price then in effect shall forthwith be readjusted to such Conversion Price as would have obtained had the adjustment which was made upon the issuance of such Option, Right or Convertible Security not exercised or converted prior to such change been made upon the basis of such change, but no further adjustment shall be made for the actual issuance of Common Stock upon the exercise or conversion of any such Option, Right or Convertible Security.

<u>Comment</u>: *The trick is to adjust the exercise price downward (it should never go up), meaning more shares for the same amount of money or securities, in proportion to the "injury." Thus, assume 100 shares of convertible preferred outstanding, designed to convert into 100 shares of common stock. To harmonize both major categories of derivatives -- convertible securities (in which the target stock is derived by handing over, or "converting" the existing security) and warrants or options (in which the target stock is paid for in cash and the derivatives expire) -- the exercise price is established as a function of a dollar amount, rather than a ratio. Thus, in the hypothetical stated, the exercise or conversion price is established (as a defined term) at ten dollars and the number of common shares into which each preferred share converts is derived by dividing ten dollars into the base number . . . in this case ten dollars, the result being share for share or 100 shares in the aggregate. In all subsequent calculations, the exercise price is adjusted (always downwards) but the base number - ten dollars (usually the liquidation preference of the preferred) - stays the same. There are a number of confusions which easily creep into the drafting of the section. For example, can the exercise price go up? The answer, as indicated, is ordinarily "no," at least by virtue of cheap stock anti-dilution. Does the exercise price which is ratcheted down always mean the original exercise price or the exercise price immediately preceding the dilutive event? The answer can vary but usually the latter is meant. Thus, if the conversion price goes down from ten dollars to, say, five dollars, a subsequent round at seven dollars doesn't budge it again. If a dilutive issuance is followed by an anti-dilutive issuance, can the two events cancel each other? Usually, the answer is "no". An adjustment in the conversion price is usually pegged to the issuance of cheap stock or the right to buy cheap stock - say another convertible security or an option. If the option lapses, is the adjustment reversed? Ordinarily, "no".*

(iv)   Adjustment of Conversion Price Upon Issuance of Additional Shares of Common Stock. In the event the Company shall at any time after the Original Issue Date issue Additional Shares of Common Stock (including Additional Shares of Common Stock deemed to be issued pursuant to Subsection 4(d)(iii), but excluding shares issued as a dividend or distribution as provided in Subsection 4(f) or upon a stock split or combination as provided in Subsection 4(e)), without consideration or for a consideration per share less than the applicable Conversion Price in effect on the date of and immediately prior to such issue, then and in such event, such Conversion Price shall be reduced, concurrently with such issue to a price (calculated to the nearest cent) determined by multiplying such Conversion Price by a fraction, (A) the numerator of which shall be (1) the number of shares of Common Stock outstanding immediately prior to such issue plus (2) the number of shares of Common Stock which the aggregate consideration received by the Company for the total number of Additional Shares of Common Stock so issued would purchase at such Conversion Price; and (B) the denominator of which shall be (1) the number of shares of Common Stock outstanding immediately prior to such issue plus (2) the number of such Additional Shares of Common Stock so issued.

> Comment: *This formula establishes what is referred to as "Weighted Average Antidilution"—the formula takes into account the extent to which the diluted shareholders are actually "injured" by the dilutive event. An alternative would be "Full Ratchet Antidilution," which simply reduces the conversion price for the diluted shareholders to the offering price of the dilutive issue.*

Notwithstanding the foregoing, the applicable Conversion Price shall not be reduced if the amount of such reduction would be an amount less than $.05, but any such amount shall be carried forward and reduction with respect thereto made at the time of and together with any subsequent reduction which, together with such amount and any other amount or amounts so carried forward, shall aggregate $.05 or more.

> Comment: *The foregoing, while complicated, does not cover every possible contingency, the trickiest being the effect of differing anti-dilution provisions in various series or classes of securities. The simplest solution is to ban all subsequent anti-dilution protection in any other security unless the Series A consents and the agreements entirely rewritten.*

> Comment: *The foregoing does not contain a 'play or pay' provision. Such provisions limit the protection of anti-dilution to those diluted shareholders who participate in the dilutive offering. Those*

participating shareholders gain the benefit of the newer, reduced price (both for the newly issued securities and for those that they already hold). Those who remain on the sidelines are not entitled to a reduction in the conversion price for their currently held securities, as an incentive for investor loyalty. More extreme versions of these provisions force conversion of non-participating shareholders, leaving them bereft of antidilution protection going forward. Play or pay provisions are company friendly, as they represent a lever for continued investment.

(v)   Determination of Consideration.   For purposes of this Subsection 4(d), the consideration received by the Company for the issue of any Additional Shares of Common Stock shall be computed as follows:

(A)   Cash   and   Property: Such consideration shall:

(I)   insofar as it consists of cash, be computed at the aggregate of cash received by the Company, excluding amounts paid or payable for accrued interest or accrued dividends;

(II)   insofar as it consists of property other than cash, be computed at the fair market value thereof at the time of such issue, as determined in good faith by the Board of Directors; and

(III)   in the event Additional Shares of Common Stock are issued together with other shares or securities or other assets of the Company for consideration which covers both, be the proportion of such consideration so received, computed as provided in clauses (I) and (II) above, as determined in good faith by the Board of Directors.

(B)   Options, Rights and Convertible Securities. The consideration per share received by the Company for Additional Shares of Common Stock deemed to have been issued pursuant to Subsection 4(d)(iii), relating to Options, Rights and Convertible Securities, shall be determined by dividing

(x)   the total amount, if any, received or receivable by the Company as consideration for the issue of such Options, Rights or Convertible Securities, plus the minimum aggregate amount of additional consideration (as set forth in the instruments relating thereto, without regard to any provision contained therein for a subsequent adjustment of such consideration) payable to the Company upon the exercise of such Options, Rights or the conversion or exchange of such Convertible Securities, by

(y)   the maximum number of shares of Common Stock (as set forth in the instruments relating thereto, without regard to any provision contained therein for a subsequent adjustment of such number) issuable upon the exercise of such Options or the conversion or exchange of such Convertible Securities.

(e)   Adjustment for Stock Splits and Combinations. If the Company shall at any time or from time to time after the Original Issue Date effect a subdivision of the outstanding Common Stock, the Conversion Price then in effect immediately before that subdivision shall be proportionately decreased. If the Company shall at any time or from time to time after the Original Issue Date combine the outstanding shares of Common Stock, the Conversion Price then in effect immediately before the combination shall be proportionately increased. Any adjustment under this paragraph shall become effective at the close of business on the date the subdivision or combination becomes effective.

(f)   Adjustment for Certain Dividends and Distributions. In the event the Company at any time, or from time to time after the Original Issue Date shall make or issue a dividend or other distribution payable in additional shares of Common Stock, then and in each such event the Conversion Price shall be decreased as of the time of such issuance, by multiplying the Conversion Price by a fraction:

(i)   the numerator of which shall be the total number of shares of Common Stock issued and outstanding immediately prior to the time of such issuance, and

(ii)   the denominator of which shall be the total number of shares of Common Stock issued and outstanding immediately prior to the time of such issuance plus the number of shares of Common Stock issuable in payment of such dividend or distribution.

(g)   Adjustments for Other Dividends and Distributions. In the event the Company at any time or from time to time after the Original

Issue Date shall make or issue a dividend or other distribution payable in securities of the Company other than shares of Common Stock, then and in each such event provision shall be made so that the holders of shares of the Series A Preferred Stock shall receive upon conversion thereof in addition to the number of shares of Common Stock receivable thereupon, the amount of securities of the Company that they would have received had their Series A Preferred Stock been converted into Common Stock on the date of such event and had thereafter, during the period from the date of such event to and including the conversion date, retained such securities receivable by them as aforesaid during such period given application to all adjustments called for during such period, under this paragraph with respect to the rights of the holders of the Series A Preferred Stock.

(h)   Adjustment for Reclassification, Exchange, or Substitution. If the Common Stock issuable upon the conversion of the Series A Preferred Stock shall be changed into the same or a different number of shares of any class or classes of stock, whether by capital reorganization, reclassification, or otherwise (other than a subdivision or combination of shares or stock dividend provided for above, or a reorganization, merger, consolidation, or sale of assets for below), then and in each such event the holder of each share of Series A Preferred Stock shall have the right thereafter to convert such shares into the kind and amount of shares of stock and other securities and property receivable upon such reorganization, reclassification, or other change, by holders of the number of shares of Common Stock into which such shares of Series A Preferred Stock might have been converted immediately prior to such reorganization, reclassification, or change, all subject to further adjustment as provided herein.

(i)   Adjustment for Merger or Reorganization, etc. In case of any consolidation or merger of the Company with or into another corporation or the sale of all or substantially all of the assets of the Company to another corporation (other than a consolidation, merger or sale which is treated as a liquidation pursuant to Subsection 2(c)), (i) if the surviving entity shall consent in writing to the following provisions, then each share of Series A Preferred Stock shall thereafter be convertible into the kind and amount of shares of stock or other securities or property to which a holder of the number of shares of Common Stock of the Company deliverable upon conversion of such Series A Preferred Stock would have been entitled upon such consolidation, merger or sale; and, in such case, appropriate adjustment (as determined in good faith by the Board of Directors) shall be made in the application of the provisions in this Section 4 set forth with respect to the rights and interest thereafter of the holders of the Series A Preferred Stock, to the end that the provisions set forth in this Section 4 (including provisions with respect to changes in and other adjustments of the Conversion Price) shall thereafter be applicable, as nearly as reasonably may be, in relation to any shares of stock or other property thereafter deliverable upon the conversion of the Series A Preferred Stock; or (ii) if the surviving entity shall not so consent, then each holder of Series A Preferred Stock may, after receipt of notice specified in subsection (l) below, elect to convert such Stock into Common Stock as provided in this Section 4 or to accept the distributions to which he or she shall be entitled under Section 2(a) through (c), assuming holders of the sixty-six and two-thirds percent (66-2/3%) of the Series A Preferred Stock have not voted, as per section 2(c), that the merger or consolidation shall not be deemed to be a liquidation.

> Comment: *This is a particularly tricky section because there are a variety of options for Series A preferred holders. Obviously, each should receive notice and be allowed to convert. Given a specific vote, should the Series A Preferred be required to convert? If offered a security which looks like the existing security, should the Series A Preferred be required to accept the same? Is a class vote on that issue required? If the Series A can treat the transaction as a liquidation, does it get only par plus accrued dividends or that amount plus a share in the pot available to the common stockholders?*

(j)   No Impairment.   The Company will not, by amendment of its Certificate of Incorporation or through any reorganization, transfer of assets, consolidation, merger, dissolution, issue or sale of securities or any other voluntary action, avoid or seek to avoid the observance or performance of any of the terms to be observed or performed hereunder by the Company, but will at all times in good faith assist in the carrying out of all the provisions of this Section 4 and in the taking of all such action as may be necessary or appropriate in order to protect the Conversion Rights of the holders of the Series A Preferred Stock against impairment.

> Comment: *Subsections (i) and (j) can be read to imply that, unless the Series A vote in favor of a non-survival merger, the surviving company must swap a similar preferred for the Series A - i.e., no squeeze out mergers absent mandatory conversion under 5(2)(ii).*

(k)   Certificate as to Adjustments.   Upon the occurrence of each adjustment or readjustment of the Conversion Price pursuant to this Section 4, the Company at its expense shall promptly compute such adjustment or readjustment in accordance with the terms hereof and furnish to each holder, if any, of Series A Preferred Stock a certificate setting forth such adjustment or readjustment and showing in detail the facts upon which such adjustment or readjustment is based and shall file a copy of such certificate with its corporate records. The Company shall, upon the written request at any time of any holder of Series A Preferred Stock, furnish or cause to be furnished to such holder a similar certificate setting forth (i) such adjustments and readjustments, (ii) the Conversion Price then in effect, and (iii) the number of shares of Common Stock and the amount, if any, of other property which then would be received upon the conversion of Series A Preferred Stock. Despite such adjustment or readjustment, the form of each or all Series A Preferred Stock Certificates, if the same shall reflect the initial or any subsequent conversion price, need not be changed in order for the adjustments or readjustments to be valued in accordance with the provisions of this Certificate of Designation, which shall control.

        (l)   Notice of Record Date. In the event:

        (i)   that the Company declares a dividend (or any other distribution) on its Common Stock payable in Common Stock or other securities of the Company;

        (ii)   that the Company subdivides or combines its outstanding shares of Common Stock;

        (iii)   of any reclassification of the Common Stock of the Company (other than a subdivision or combination of its outstanding shares of Common Stock or a stock dividend or stock distribution thereon), or of any consolidation or merger of the Company into or with another corporation, or of the sale of all or substantially all of the assets of the Company; or

        (iv)   of the involuntary or voluntary dissolution, liquidation or winding up of the Company;

then the Company shall cause to be filed at its principal office or at the office of the transfer agent of the Series A Preferred Stock, and shall cause to be mailed to the holders of the Series A Preferred Stock at their last addresses as shown on the records of the Company or such transfer agent, at least ten (10) days prior to the record date specified in (A) below or twenty (20) days before the date specified in (B) below, a notice stating

        (A)   the record date of such dividend, distribution, subdivision or combination, or, if a record is not to be taken, the date as of which the holders of Common Stock of record to be entitled to such dividend, distribution, subdivision or combination are to be determined, or

(B)   the   date   on   which   such
reclassification, consolidation, merger, sale, dissolution, liquidation or
winding up is expected to become effective, and the date as of which it
is expected that holders of Common Stock of record shall be entitled to
exchange their shares of Common Stock for securities or other property
deliverable upon such reclassification, consolidation, merger, sale,
dissolution or winding up.

5.   Mandatory Conversion.

(a)   The Company may, at its option, require all (and not
less than all) holders of shares of Series A Preferred Stock then outstanding to
convert their shares of Series A Preferred Stock into shares of Common Stock,
at the then effective conversion rate pursuant to Section 4, at any time on or
after (1) the closing of the sale of shares of Common Stock, at a price per share
which exceeds 300 percent of the Conversion Price then in effect, in a fully
underwritten public offering pursuant to an effective registration statement
under the Securities Act of 1933, as amended, other than a registration relating
solely to a transaction under Rule 145 under such Act (or any successor thereto)
or to an employee benefit plan of the Company, underwritten by a reputable
underwriter acceptable to the holders of a majority of the then outstanding
Series A Preferred Stock, resulting in at least $[_____] of gross proceeds
to the Company, or (ii), the conversion into Common Stock of a majority of the
outstanding shares of Series A Preferred Stock; on such date as less than _____
shares of Series A Preferred Stock shall be outstanding.

Comment: *The test establishing a 300% of Conversion Price
benchmark can be ambiguous if, as is often the case, an IPO is
preceded by a stock split or a reverse stock split in order to get the
public offering price right.*

(b)   All holders of record of shares of Series A Preferred
Stock then outstanding will be given at least ten (10) days' prior written notice
of the date fixed and the place designated for mandatory or special conversion
of all such shares of Series A Preferred Stock pursuant to this Section 5. Such
notice will be sent by first class or registered mail, postage prepaid, to each
record holder of Series A Preferred Stock at such holder's address last shown on
the records of the transfer agent for the Series A Preferred Stock (or the records
of the Company, if it serves as its own transfer agent).

6.   Redemption of the Series A Preferred Stock.

Comment: *See Treatise §13.6 for the problems occasioned
by § 305 of the Internal Revenue Code if a redemption premium is*

involved in the redemption price. For other issues (such as the problems SBICs have in investing in redeemable preferred), see 1 Halloran 7-22.

(a)   If, on [date 10 years from execution of this document], any shares of Series A Preferred Stock shall be then outstanding, the Company shall have the right to redeem (unless otherwise prevented by law) all (but not less than all) such outstanding shares at an amount per share equal to $10 plus an amount equal to accrued but unpaid dividends, if any, to the date of redemption on such share.

(b)   Sixty (60) days' prior notice by the Company of the exercise of the redemption option pursuant to Section 6(a) of this Section 6 shall be sent by first-class certified mail, postage prepaid and return receipt requested, by the Company to the holders of the shares of Series A Preferred Stock to be redeemed at their respective addresses as the same shall appear on the books of the Company.

(c)   On or prior to each Redemption Date, the Company shall deposit the Redemption Price of all shares of Series A Preferred Stock designated for redemption in the redemption notice and not yet redeemed with a bank or trust corporation having aggregate capital and surplus in excess of [$100,000,000] as a trust fund for the benefit of the respective holders of the shares designated for redemption and not yet redeemed, with irrevocable instructions and authority to the bank or trust corporation to pay the Redemption Price for such shares to their respective holders on or after the Redemption Date upon receipt of notification from the Company that such holder has surrendered his share certificate to the Company pursuant to Section 6(b) above. As of the Redemption Date, the deposit shall constitute full payment of the shares to their holders, and from and after the Redemption Date the shares so called for redemption shall be redeemed and shall be deemed to be no longer outstanding, and the holders thereof shall cease to be stockholders with respect to such shares and shall have no rights with respect thereto except the rights to receive from the bank or trust corporation payment of the Redemption Price of the shares, without interest, upon surrender of their certificates therefor. Such instructions shall also provide that any moneys deposited by the Company pursuant to this Section 6(c) for the redemption of shares thereafter converted into shares of the Company's Common Stock pursuant to Section 6(e) hereof prior to the Redemption Date shall be returned to the Company forthwith upon such conversion. The balance of any moneys deposited by the Company pursuant to this Section 6(c) remaining unclaimed at the expiration of two (2) years following the Redemption Date shall thereafter be returned to the Company upon its request expressed in a resolution of its Board of Directors.

(d)   If upon the Mandatory Redemption Date the assets of the Company available for redemption are insufficient to pay the holders of outstanding shares of Series A Preferred Stock the full amounts to which they are entitled, such holders of shares of Series A Preferred Stock shall share ratably according to the respective amounts which would be payable in respect of such shares to be redeemed by the holders thereof, if all amounts payable on or with respect to such shares were paid in full. The unpaid balance of the amounts payable in respect of such redeemed shares shall be paid to each redeeming shareholders in the form of a promissory note, in the principal amount equal to the unpaid balance due that redeeming shareholder. Such notes shall bear no interest, and shall be payable in five (5) equal annual installments.

(e)   Optional Redemption.

(i)   Upon the occurrence of any Optional Redemption Event the Company will, by notice given to each holder of Series A Preferred Stock, offer to redeem all (but not fewer than all) shares of Series A Preferred Stock then owned by such holder at a price equal to:

108.000% of the Mandatory Redemption Price if such offer to redeem is made prior to July 1, 2000;

106.667% of the Mandatory Redemption Price if such offer to redeem is made subsequent to June 30, 2000 and prior to July 1, 2001;

105.334% of the Mandatory Redemption Price if such offer to redeem is made subsequent to June 30, 2001 and prior to July 1, 2002;

104.001% of the Mandatory Redemption Price if such offer to redeem is made subsequent to June 30, 2002 and prior to July 1, 2003;

102.668% of the Mandatory Redemption Price if such offer to redeem is made subsequent to June 30, 2003 and prior to July 1, 2004;

101.335% of the Mandatory Redemption Price if such offer to redeem is made subsequent to June 30, 2004 and prior to July 1, 2005.

(ii)   Upon receipt of a notice given pursuant to Section 6(d), each holder of Series A Preferred Stock shall have the right to accept such offer by tendering such holder's shares to the Company for redemption, at an address to be set forth in such notice, at any time prior to 5:00 p.m. New York City time on the 15th day following the making of the offer to redeem by notice given as prescribed herein.

(iii)   The following shall be Optional Redemption Events:

(A)   the failure, for any reason, of the Company to have received a total consideration of at least $5,000,000 in respect of the sale of shares of Series A Preferred Stock before December 31, 2000; provided, however, that if, through no fault of the Company, a purchaser who has subscribed for shares of Series A Preferred Stock fails or refuses to purchase the number of Series A Preferred Stock it has subscribed for, the Company shall have ninety (90) days from the date of notice to the Company of such failure or refusal to find a qualified replacement purchaser;

(B)   the occurrence of a Change of Control, which shall be deemed to have occurred if:

1.   any person or group of related or affiliated persons shall have become the beneficial owner or owners of forty percent (40%) or more of the outstanding voting stock of the Company; provided, that beneficial ownership of Series A Preferred Stock shall not be given effect toward counting a person's or group of related or affiliated persons' beneficial ownership;

2.   there shall have occurred a merger or consolidation in which the Company is not the survivor or in which holders of Common Stock of the Company shall have become entitled to receive cash, securities of the Company other than voting common stock or securities of any other person; or

3.   at any time a majority of the members of the Board of Directors of the Company shall be persons who were elected at one or more meetings held, or by one or more consents given, by the stockholders of the Company during the preceding twelve (12) months and who were not

members of the Board of Directors twelve (12) months prior to that time;

(C)   if the Company shall take any action referred to in *[insert here reference to social covenants, either included in Certificate of Designation or part of a separate document (the Shareholders Agreement, or a Stock Purchase Agreement, for example) (weigh here the pros and cons of attaching such a document, or incorporating it by reference, to the Certificate, given that the Certificate will be a matter of public record, and difficult to change; pros are precisely that, cons are more subtle, and involve hesitation concerning revealing too much about the company). Breach of the covenants trigger redemption at the discretion of the Series A Preferred Shareholders.]* without having obtained the required consent of the holders of Series A Preferred Stock.

(f)   Cancellation of Redeemed Stock.   Any shares of Series A Preferred Stock redeemed pursuant to this Section or otherwise acquired by the Company in any manner whatsoever shall be canceled and shall not under any circumstances be reissued; and the Company may from time to time take such appropriate corporate action as may be necessary to reduce accordingly the number of authorized shares of the Company's capital stock.

(g)   The Company will not, and will not permit any subsidiary of the Company to, purchase or acquire any shares of Series A Preferred Stock otherwise than pursuant to (A) the terms of this Section or (B) an offer made on the same terms to all holders of Series A Preferred Stock at the time outstanding.

(h)   Anything contained in this Section 6 to the contrary notwithstanding, the holders of shares of Series A Preferred Stock to be redeemed in accordance with this Section 6 shall have the right, exercisable at any time up to the close of business on the applicable redemption date (unless the Company is legally prohibited form redeeming such shares on such date, in which event such right shall be exercisable until the removal of such legal disability), to convert all or any part of such shares to be redeemed as herein provided into shares of Common Stock pursuant to Section 4 hereof.

7.   Sinking Fund.

There shall be no sinking fund for the payment of dividends, or liquidation preferences on the Series A Preferred Stock or the redemption of any shares thereof.

8.   Amendment.

This Certificate of Designation constitutes an agreement between the Company and the holders of the Series A Preferred Stock. It may be amended by vote of the Board of Directors of the Company and the holders of a majority of the outstanding shares of Series A Preferred Stock.

IN WITNESS WHEREOF, the Company has caused this Certificate to be executed by its President and attested to by its Secretary this ___ day of _____, 199_.

[   ]
(   )

By: _____
President

ATTEST:

_____
Secretary

[Seal]

NEWCO, INC.

REGISTRATION RIGHTS AGREEMENT

This Agreement is made as of _____, 199_, by and among Newco, Inc., a Delaware corporation (the "Company"), and the persons and entities listed on the signature pages hereof (the "Stockholders"), who include (i) a majority [or all] of the holders of the common stock ("Common Stock") of the Company and (ii) the persons named as Investors in the Company's Convertible Preferred Stock pursuant to the Stock Purchase Agreement of even date (the "Convertible Agreement").

PREAMBLE

In light of the fact the Company and the Holders desire to extend registration rights to the Investors in the Company's Convertible Preferred Stock pursuant to the Stock Purchase Agreement the Company and the Stockholders desire to amend the registration rights provisions set forth in the registration rights agreement dated _____ (the "Prior Registration Rights Agreement"), to amend and restate in this Agreement the obligations with respect to registration rights, which shall for all purposes subsume, supersede and replace the Prior Registration Rights Agreement.

NOW, THEREFORE, in consideration of the premises and mutual agreements set forth herein, the Company and the Holders agree as follows:

Section 1. <u>Definitions</u>. As used in this Agreement, the following terms shall have the following meanings:

(a) "Commission" shall mean the Securities and Exchange Commission, or any other federal agency at the time administering the Securities Act.

(b) "Exchange Act" shall mean the Securities Exchange Act of 1934, as amended, or any similar Federal statute and the rules and regulations thereunder, all as the same shall be in effect at the time.

(c)   "Holder" shall mean any holder of outstanding Registrable Securities or anyone who holds outstanding Registrable Securities to whom the registration rights conferred by this Agreement have been transferred in compliance with this Agreement.

(d)   "Initiating Holders" shall mean any Holder or Holders of at least fifty-one percent (51%) of the Registrable Securities then outstanding.

(e)   "Register," "registered" and "registration" shall refer to a registration effected by preparing and filing a registration statement in compliance with the Securities Act, and the declaration or ordering of the effectiveness of such registration statement, and compliance with applicable state securities laws of such states in which Holders notify the Company of their intention to offer Registrable Securities.

(f)   "Registrable Securities" shall mean all of the following to the extent the same have not been sold to the public (i) any and all shares of Common Stock of the Company issued or issuable upon conversion of shares of the Company's Convertible Preferred Stock; or (ii) stock issued in respect of stock referred to in (i) above in any reorganization; or (iii) stock issued in respect of the stock referred to in (i) or (ii) as a result of a stock split, stock dividend, recapitalization or combination.   Notwithstanding the foregoing, Registrable Securities shall not include otherwise Registrable Securities (i) sold by a person in a transaction in which his rights under this Agreement are not properly assigned; or (ii) (A) sold to or through a broker or dealer or underwriter in a public distribution or a public securities transaction, or (B) sold in a transaction exempt from the registration and prospectus delivery requirements of the Securities Act under Section 4(1) thereof so that all transfer restrictions, and restrictive legends with respect thereto, if any, are removed upon the consummation of such sale or (C) the registration rights associated with such securities have been terminated pursuant to Section 16 of this Agreement.

(g)   "Rule 144" shall mean Rule 144 under the Securities Act or any successor or similar rule as may be enacted by the Commission from time to time, but shall not include Rule 144A.

(h)   "Rule 144A" shall mean Rule 144A under the Securities Act or any successor or similar rule as may be enacted by the Commission from time to time, but shall not include Rule 144.

(i)   "Securities Act" shall mean the Securities Act of 1933, as amended, or any similar Federal statute and the rules and regulations thereunder, all as the same shall be in effect at the time.

Section 2.   Restrictions   on   Transferability.   The   Registrable
Securities (as defined herein) shall not be sold, assigned, transferred or pledged
except upon the conditions specified in this Agreement, which conditions are
intended to ensure compliance with the provisions of the Securities Act. Each
Holder will cause any proposed purchaser, assignee, transferee, or pledgee of
the Registrable Securities held by a Holder to agree to take and hold such
securities subject to the provisions and upon the conditions specified in this
Agreement.

Section 3.   Restrictive   Legend.   Each   certificate   representing
Registrable Securities shall (unless other permitted by the provisions of Section 4
below) be stamped or otherwise imprinted with a legend substantially in the
following form (in addition to any legend required under applicable state securities
laws or otherwise):

> THE SHARES REPRESENTED BY THIS
> CERTIFICATE HAVE BEEN ACQUIRED
> FOR INVESTMENT AND HAVE NOT
> BEEN   REGISTERED   UNDER   THE
> SECURITIES ACT OF 1933.   THESE
> SHARES   MAY   NOT   BE   SOLD   OR
> TRANSFERRED IN THE ABSENCE OF
> SUCH   REGISTRATION   OR   AN
> EXEMPTION THEREFROM UNDER SAID
> ACT.   COPIES OF THE AGREEMENTS
> COVERING THE PURCHASE OF THESE
> SHARES AND RIGHTS TO REGISTER
> THESE   SHARES   AND   RESTRICTING
> THEIR TRANSFER MAY BE OBTAINED
> AT NO COST BY WRITTEN REQUEST
> MADE BY THE HOLDER OF RECORD
> OF   THIS   CERTIFICATE   TO   THE
> SECRETARY OF THE CORPORATION
> AT   THE   PRINCIPAL   EXECUTIVE
> OFFICES OF THE CORPORATION.

Each Holder consents to the Company making a notation on its records
and giving instructions to any transfer agent of the Registrable Securities in order
to implement the restrictions on transfer established in this Agreement.

Section 4.   Notice of Proposed Transfer.   The Holder of each
certificate representing Registrable Securities, by acceptance thereof, agrees to
comply in all respects with the provisions of this Section 4. Each such Holder
agrees not to make any disposition of all or any portion of any Registrable
Securities unless and until:

(a)   There is in effect a registration statement under the Securities Act covering such proposed disposition and such disposition is made in accordance with such registration statement; or

(b)   (i)   Such Holder shall have notified the Company of the proposed disposition and shall have furnished the Company with a detailed statement of the circumstances surrounding the proposed disposition, and

(ii)   If reasonably by the Company, such Holder shall furnish the Company with an opinion of counsel, reasonably satisfactory to the Company that such disposition shall not require registration of such shares under the Securities Act. It is agreed, however, that no such opinion will be required for Rule 144 or Rule 144A transactions, except in unusual circumstances.

(c)   Notwithstanding the provisions of paragraphs (a) and (b) above, no such registration statement or opinion of counsel shall be necessary for a transfer by a Holder which is a partnership to a partner of such partnership or a retired partner of such partnership who retires after the date hereof, or to the estate of any such partner or retired partner or the transfer by gift, will or intestate succession of any partner to his spouse or siblings, lineal descendants or ancestors of such partner or spouse, provided, that such transferee agrees in writing to be subject to all of the terms hereof to the same extent as if he were an original Holder hereunder.

Section 5.   Requested Registration.

(a)   If the Company shall receive from Initiating Holders a written request that the Company effect any registration with respect to all or at least 33-1/3% of the issued and outstanding Registrable Securities held by Initiating Holders, the Company shall:

(i)   promptly give written notice of the proposed registration to all other Holders; and

(ii)   as soon as practicable use its best efforts to register (including, without limitation, the execution of an undertaking to file post-effective amendments and any other governmental requirements) all Registrable Securities which the Initiating Holders request to be registered within twenty (20) days after receipt of such written notice from the Company; provided, that the Company shall not be obligated to file a registration statement pursuant to this Section 5:

(A)   prior to June 30, 199_;

(B)   in any particular state in which the Company would be required to execute a general consent to service of process in effecting such registration;

(C)   within 120 days following the effective date of any registered offering of the Company's securities to the general public in which the Holders of Registrable Securities shall have been able effectively to register all Registrable Securities as to which registration shall have been requested;

(D)   in any registration having an aggregate offering price (before deduction of underwriting discounts and expenses of sale) of less than $5,000,000; or

(E)   after the Company has effected one such registration pursuant to this Section 5 and such registration has been declared or ordered effective, except as provided in Section 6.

Subject to the foregoing clauses (A) through (E), the Company shall file a registration statement covering the Registrable Securities so requested to be registered as soon as practical, but in any event within ninety (90) days after receipt of the request or requests of the Initiating Holders and shall use reasonable best efforts to have such registration statement promptly declared effective by the Commission whether or not all Registrable Securities requested to be registered can be included; provided, however, that if the Company shall furnish to such Holders a certificate signed by the President of the Company stating that in the good faith judgment of the Board of Directors it would be seriously detrimental to the Company and its shareholders for such registration statement to be filed within such ninety-day (90-day) period and it is therefore essential to defer the filing of such registration statement, the Company shall have an additional period of not more than ninety (90) days after the expiration of the initial ninety-day (90-day) period within which to file such registration statement; provided, that during such time the Company may not file a registration statement for securities to be issued and sold for its own account.

(b)   If the Initiating Holders intend to distribute the Registrable Securities covered by their request by means of an underwriting, they shall so advise the Company as a part of their request. In such event or if an underwriting is required by subsection 5(c), the Company shall include such information in the written notice referred to in subsection 5(a)(i). In either such event, if so requested in writing by the Company, the Initiating Holders shall negotiate with an underwriter selected by the Company with regard to the underwriting of such requested registration; provided, however, that if a majority in interest of the Initiating Holders have not agreed with such underwriter as to the terms and conditions of such underwriting within twenty (20) days following commencement of such negotiations, a majority in interest of the Initiating Holders may select an underwriter of their choice. The right of any Holder to registration pursuant to Section 5 shall be conditioned upon such Holder's participation in such underwriting and the inclusion of such Holder's Registrable Securities in the underwriting (unless otherwise mutually agreed by a majority in interest of the Initiating Holders and such Holder) to the extent provided herein. The Company shall (together with all Holders proposing to distribute their securities through such underwriting) enter into an underwriting agreement in customary form with the underwriter or underwriters selected for such underwriting. Notwithstanding any other provision of this Section 5, if the managing underwriter advises the Initiating Holders in writing that marketing factors require a limitation of the number of shares to be underwritten, the Company shall so advise all Holders, and the number of shares of Registrable Securities that may be included in the registration and underwriting shall be allocated among all Holders thereof in proportion, as nearly as practicable, to the respective amounts of Registrable Securities held by such Holders; provided, however, that securities to be included in such registration statement as a result of piggyback registration rights as well as any securities to be offered by the Company, its officers and employees shall be excluded from the registration statement prior to the exclusion of any Registrable Securities held by the Holders. If any Holder disapproves of the terms of the underwriting, he may elect to withdraw therefrom by written notice to the Company, the managing underwriter and the Initiating Holders. If, by the withdrawal of such Registrable Securities, a greater number of Registrable Securities held by other Holders may be included in such registration (up to the limit imposed by the underwriters) the Company shall offer to all Holders who have included Registrable Securities in the registration the right to include additional Registrable Securities in the same proportion used in determining the limitation   as set forth above.   Any Registrable Securities which are excluded from the underwriting by reason of the underwriter's marketing limitation or withdrawn from such underwriting shall be withdrawn from such registration.

(c)   If the Company is subject to the reporting requirements of Section 13 or 15 of the Exchange Act as a result of the registration of shares of its Common Stock under the Exchange Act, any registration pursuant to this Section 5   must be firmly underwritten if the registration exceeds two percent (2%) of the Company's outstanding Common Stock on an as-converted basis.

Section 6.   Piggyback Registration.

(a)   If at any time or from time to time, the Company shall determine to register any of its securities, for its own account or the account of any of its shareholders, other than a registration relating solely to employee benefit plans, or a registration relating solely to an SEC Rule 145 transaction, a transaction relating solely to the sale of debt or convertible debt instruments or a registration on any form (other than Form S-1, S-2 or S-3, or their successor forms) which does not include substantially the same information as would be required to be included in a registration statement covering the sale of Registrable Securities, the Company will:

(i)   give to each Holder written notice thereof as soon as practicable prior to filing the registration statement; and

(ii)   include in such registration and in any underwriting involved therein, all the Registrable Securities specified in a written request or requests, made within fifteen (15) days after receipt of such written notice from the Company, by any Holder or Holders, except as set forth in subsection (b) below.

(b)   If the registration is for a registered public offering involving an underwriting, the Company shall so advise the Holders as a part of the written notice given pursuant to subsection 6(a)(i). In such event, the right of any Holder to registration pursuant to Section 6 shall be conditioned upon such Holder's participation in such underwriting and the inclusion of such Holder's Registrable Securities in the underwriting to the extent provided herein. All Holders proposing to distribute their securities through such underwriting shall (together with the Company and the other holders distributing their securities through such underwriting) enter into an underwriting agreement in customary form with the underwriter or underwriters selected for such underwriting by the Company. Notwithstanding any other provision of this Section 6, if the managing underwriter determines that marketing factors require a limitation of the number of shares to be underwritten, the managing underwriter may limit the number of Registrable Securities to be included in the registration and underwriting, or may exclude Registrable Securities entirely from such registration if the registration is the first registered offering for the sale of the Company's securities to the general public (provided that no shares held by officers and directors of the Company, other than Registrable Securities that may be owned by officers and directors, are included in the registration and underwriting). The Company shall so advise all Holders and the other Holders distributing their securities through such underwriting pursuant to piggy-back registration rights similar to this Section 6, and the number of shares of Registrable Securities and other securities that may be included in the registration and underwriting shall be allocated among all Holders and other holders in proportion, as nearly as practicable, to the respective amounts of Registrable Securities held by such Holders and other securities held by other holders at the time of filing the registration statement. If any Holder disapproves of the terms of any such underwriting, he may elect to withdraw therefrom by written notice to the Company and the managing underwriter. If, by the withdrawal of such Registrable Securities, a greater number of Registrable Securities held by other Holders may be included in such registration (up to the limit imposed by the underwriters), the Company shall offer to all Holders who have included Registrable Securities in the registration the right to include additional Registrable Securities.   Any Registrable Securities excluded or withdrawn from such underwriting shall be withdrawn from such registration.

Section 7.   Form S-3.   The Company shall use its best efforts to qualify for registration on Form S-3 or its successor form.   After the Company has qualified for the use of Form S-3, Initiating Holders shall have the right at any time to request registrations on Form S-3 (such requests shall be in writing and shall state the number of shares of Registrable Securities to be disposed of and the intended method of disposition of shares by such Holders), subject only to the following:

(a)   The Company shall not be required to file a registration statement pursuant to this Section 7 within ninety (90) days of the effective date of any registration referred to in Sections 5 and 6 above.

(b)   The Company shall not be required to file a registration statement pursuant to this Section 7 unless the Holder or Holders requesting registration propose to dispose of shares of Registrable Securities having an aggregate disposition price (before deduction of underwriting discounts and expenses of sale) of at least $1,000,000.

(c)   The Company shall not be required to file more than two registration statements pursuant to this Section 7 within any twelve-month period.

The Company shall give written notice to all Holders of Registrable Securities of the receipt of a request for registration pursuant to this Section 7 and shall provide a reasonable opportunity for other Holders to participate in the registration; provided, that if the registration is for an underwritten offering, the following terms shall apply to all participants in such offering: The right of any Holder to registration pursuant to Section 7 shall be conditioned upon such Holder's participation in such underwriting and the inclusion of such Holder's Registrable Securities in the underwriting to the extent provided herein.   All Holders proposing to distribute their securities through such underwriting shall (together with the Company and the other Holders distributing their securities through such underwriting) enter into an underwriting agreement in customary form with the underwriter or underwriters selected for such underwriting by the Company. Notwithstanding any other provision of this Section 7, if the managing underwriter determines that marketing factors require a limitation of the number of shares to be underwritten, the managing underwriter may limit the number of Registrable Securities to be included in the registration and underwriting. The Company shall so advise all Holders of Registrable Securities which would otherwise be registered and underwritten pursuant hereto, and the number of shares of Registrable Securities that may be included in the registration and underwriting shall be allocated among the Holders in proportion, as nearly as practicable, to the respective amounts of securities requested by such Holders to be included in such registration. If any Holder disapproves of the terms of any such underwriting, he may elect to withdraw therefrom by written notice to the Company and the underwriter. If, by the withdrawal of such Registrable Securities, a greater number of Registrable Securities held by other Holders may be included in such registration (up to the limit imposed by the underwriters), the Company shall offer to all Holders who have included Registrable Securities in the registration the right to include additional Registrable Securities in the same proportion used in determining the limitation as set forth above. Any Registrable Securities excluded or withdrawn from such underwriting shall be withdrawn from such registration. Subject to the foregoing, the Company will use its best efforts to effect promptly the registration of all shares of Registrable Securities on Form S-3 to the extent requested by the Holder or Holders thereof for purposes of disposition.

Section 8.   Expenses of Registration.   In addition to the fees and expenses contemplated by Section 9 hereof, all expenses incurred in connection with one registration pursuant to Section 5 hereof and all registrations pursuant to Sections 6 and 7 hereof, including without limitation all registration, filing and qualification fees, printing expenses, fees and disbursements of counsel for the Company and expenses of any special audits of the Company's financial statements incidental to or required by such registration, shall be borne by the Company, except that the Company shall not be required to pay underwriters' fees, discounts or commissions relating to Registrable Securities or fees of a separate legal counsel of a Holder.

Section 9.   Registration Procedures.   In the case of each registration effected by the Company pursuant to this Agreement, the Company will keep each Holder participating therein advised in writing as to the initiation of each registration and as to the completion thereof. At its expense the Company will:

(a)   keep such registration pursuant to Sections 5, 6 and 7 continuously effective for periods of one hundred twenty (120), ninety (90) and ninety (90) days, respectively, or, in each case, such reasonable period necessary to permit the Holder or Holders to complete the distribution described in the registration statement relating thereto, whichever first occurs;

(b)   promptly prepare and file with the Commission such amendments and supplements to such registration statement and the prospectus used in connection therewith as may be necessary to comply with the provisions of the Securities Act, and to keep such registration statement effective for that period of time specified in Section 9(a) above;

(c)   furnish such number of prospectuses and other documents incident thereto as a Holder from time to time may reasonably request;

(d)   use reasonable best efforts to obtain the withdrawal of any order suspending the effectiveness of a registration statement, or the lifting of any suspension of the qualification of any of the Registrable Securities for sale in any jurisdiction, at the earliest possible moment;

(e)   subject to Section 5(a)(ii)(B), register or qualify such Registrable Securities for offer and sale under the securities or Blue Sky laws of such jurisdictions as any Holder or underwriter reasonably requires, and keep such registration or qualification effective during the period set forth in Section 9(a) above;

(f)   cause all Registrable Securities covered by such registrations to be listed on each securities exchange, including NASDAQ, on which similar securities issued by the Company are then listed or, if no such listing exists, use reasonable best efforts to list all Registrable Securities on one of the New York Stock Exchanges the American Stock Exchange or NASDAQ; and

(g)   cause its accountants to issue to the underwriter, if any, or the Holders, if there is no underwriter, comfort letters and updates thereof, in customary form and covering matters of the type customarily covered in such letters with respect to underwritten offerings;

(h)   enter into such customary agreements (including underwriting agreements in customary form) and take all such other actions as the holders of a majority of the Registrable Securities being sold or the underwriters, if any, reasonably, request in order to expedite or facilitate the disposition of such Registrable Securities (including, without limitation, effecting a stock split or a combination of shares);

(i)   make available for inspection by any seller of Registrable Securities, any underwriter participating in any disposition pursuant to such registration statement, and any attorney, accountant or other agent retained by any such seller or underwriter, all financial and other records, pertinent corporate documents and properties of the Company, and cause the Company's officers, directors, employees and independent accountants to supply all information reasonably requested by any such seller, underwriter, attorney, accountant or agent in connection with such registration statement; and

(j)   if the offering is underwritten, at the request of any Holder of Registrable Securities to furnish on the date that Registrable Securities are delivered to the underwriters for sale pursuant to such registration: (i) an opinion dated such date of counsel representing the Company for the purposes of such registration, addressed to the underwriters and to such Holder, stating that such registration statement has become effective under the Securities Act and that (A) to the best knowledge of such counsel, no stop order suspending the effectiveness thereof has been issued and no proceedings for that purpose have been instituted or are pending or contemplated under the Securities Act, (B) the registration statement, the related prospectus and each amendment or supplement thereof comply as to form in all material respects with the requirements of the Securities Act (except that such counsel need not express any opinion as to financial statements or other financial data contained therein) and (C) to such other effects as reasonably may be requested by counsel for the underwriters or by such Holder or its counsel and (ii) a letter dated such date from the independent public accountants retained by the Company, addressed to the underwriters and to such seller, stating that they are independent public accountants within the meaning of the Securities Act and that, in the opinion of such accountants, the financial statements of the Company included in the registration statement or the prospectus, or any amendment or supplement thereof, comply as to form in all material respects with the applicable accounting requirements of the Securities Act, and such letter shall additionally cover such other financial matters (including information as to the period ending no more than five business days prior to the date of such letter) with respect to such registration as such underwriters reasonably may request; and

(k)   notify each Holder, at any time a prospectus covered by such registration statement is required to be delivered under the Securities Act, of the happening of any event of which it has knowledge as a result of which the prospectus included in such registration statement, as then in effect, includes an untrue statement of a material fact or omits to state a material fact required to be stated therein or necessary to make the statements therein not misleading in the light of the circumstances then existing; and

(l)   take such other actions as shall be reasonably requested by any Holder.

Section 10.   Indemnification.

(a)   In the event of a registration of any of the Registrable Securities under the Securities Act pursuant to Sections 5, 6 or 7, the Company will indemnify and hold harmless each Holder of such Registrable Securities thereunder, each underwriter of such Registrable Securities thereunder and each other person, if any, who controls such Holder or underwriter within the meaning of the Securities Act, against any losses, claims, damages or liabilities, joint or several, to which such Holder, underwriter or controlling person may become subject under the Securities Act or otherwise, insofar as such losses, claims, damages or liabilities (or actions in respect thereof) arise out of or are based upon any untrue statement or alleged untrue statement of any material fact contained in any registration statement under which such Registrable Securities were registered under the Securities Act, any preliminary prospectus or final prospectus contained therein, or any amendment or supplement thereof, or arise out of or are based upon the omission or alleged omission to state therein a material fact required to be stated therein or necessary to make the statements therein not misleading, or any violation by the Company of any rule or regulation promulgated under the Securities Act or any state securities law applicable to the Company and relating to action or inaction required of the Company in connection with any such registration, and will reimburse each such Holder, each of its officers, directors and partners, and each person controlling such Holder, each such underwriter and each person who controls any such underwriter, for any reasonable legal and any other expenses incurred in connection with investigating, defending or settling any such claim, loss, damage, liability or action, provided that the Company will not be liable in any such case to the extent that any such claim, loss, damage or liability arises out of or is based on any untrue statement or omission based upon written information furnished to the Company by an instrument duly executed by such Holder or underwriter specifically for use therein.

(b)   Each Holder will, if Registrable Securities held by or issuable to such Holder are included in the securities as to which such registration is being effected, indemnify and hold harmless the Company, each of its directors and officers, each underwriter, if any, of the Company's securities covered by such a registration statement, each person who controls the Company and each underwriter within the meaning of the Securities Act, and each other such Holder, each of its officers, directors and partners and each person controlling such Holder, against all claims, losses, expenses, damages and liabilities (or actions in respect thereof) arising out of or based on any untrue statement (or alleged untrue statement) of a material fact contained in any such registration statement, prospectus, offering circular or other document, or any omission (or alleged omission) to state therein a material fact required to be stated therein or necessary to make the statements therein not misleading, and will reimburse the Company, such Holders, such directors, officers, partners, persons or underwriters for any reasonable legal or any other expenses incurred in connection with investigating, defending or settling any such claim, loss, damage, liability or action, in each case to the extent, but only to the extent, that such untrue statement (or alleged untrue statement) or omission (or alleged omission) is made in such registration statement, prospectus, offering circular or other document in reliance upon and in conformity with written information furnished to the Company by an instrument duly executed by such Holder specifically for use therein; provided, however, the total amount for which any Holder, its officers, directors and partners, and any person controlling such Holder, shall be liable under this Section 10(b) shall not in any event exceed the aggregate proceeds received by such Holder from the sale of Registrable Securities sold by such Holder in such registration.

(c)   Each party entitled to indemnification under this Section 10 (the "Indemnified Party") shall give notice to the party required to provide indemnification (the "Indemnifying Party") promptly after such Indemnified Party has actual knowledge of any claims as to which indemnity may be sought, and shall permit the Indemnifying Party to assume the defense of any such claim or any litigation resulting therefrom, provided that counsel for the Indemnifying Party, who shall conduct the defense of such claim or litigation, shall be approved by the Indemnified Party (whose approval shall not be unreasonably withheld), and the Indemnified Party may participate in such defense at such party's expense, and provided further that the failure of any Indemnified Party to give notice as provided herein shall not relieve the Indemnifying Party of its obligations hereunder, unless such failure resulted in actual detriment to the Indemnifying Party. No Indemnifying Party, in the defense of any such claim or litigation, shall, except with the consent of each Indemnified Party, consent to entry of any judgment or enter into any settlement which does not include as an unconditional term thereof the giving by the claimant or plaintiff to such Indemnified Party of a release from all liability in respect of such claim or litigation.

(d)   Notwithstanding the foregoing, to the extent that the provisions on indemnification contained in the underwriting agreements entered into among the selling Holders, the Company and the underwriters in connection with the underwritten public offering are in conflict with the foregoing provisions, the provisions in the underwriting agreement shall be controlling as to the Registrable Securities included in the public offering; provided, however, that if, as a result of this Section 10(d), any Holder, its officers, directors, and partners and any person controlling such Holder is held liable for an amount which exceeds the aggregate proceeds received by such Holder from the sale of Registrable Securities included in a registration, as provided in Section 10(b) above, pursuant to such underwriting agreement (the "Excess Liability"), the Company shall reimburse any such Holder for such Excess Liability.

(e)   If the indemnification provided for in this Section 10 is held by a court of competent jurisdiction to be unavailable to an indemnified party with respect to any loss, liability, claim, damage or expense referred to therein, then the indemnifying party, in lieu of indemnifying such indemnified party thereunder, shall contribute to the amount paid or payable by such indemnified party as a result of such loss, liability, claim, damage or expense in such proportion as is appropriate to reflect the relative fault of the indemnifying party on the one hand and of the indemnified party on the other hand in connection with the statements or omissions which resulted in such loss, liability, claim, damage or expense as well as any other relevant equitable considerations. The relevant fault of the indemnifying party and the indemnified party shall be determined by reference to, among other things, whether the untrue or alleged untrue statement of a material fact or the omission to state a material fact relates to information supplied by the indemnifying party or by the indemnified party and the parties' relative intent, knowledge, access to information and opportunity to correct or prevent such statement or omission. Notwithstanding the foregoing, the amount any Holder shall be obligated to contribute pursuant to this Section 10(e) shall be limited to an amount equal to the proceeds to such Holder of the Restricted Securities sold pursuant to the registration statement which gives rise to such obligation to contribute (less the aggregate amount of any damages which the Holder has otherwise been required to pay in respect of such loss, claim, damage, liability or action or any substantially similar loss, claim, damage, liability or action arising from the sale of such Restricted Securities).

(f)   Survival of Indemnity. The indemnification provided by this Section 10 shall be a continuing right to indemnification and shall survive the registration and sale of any securities by any Person entitled to indemnification hereunder and the expiration or termination of this Agreement.

Section 11.   Lockup Agreement. In consideration for the Company agreeing to its obligations under this Agreement, each Holder agrees in connection with any registration of the Company's securities (whether or not such Holder is participating in such registration) upon the request of the Company and the underwriters managing any underwritten offering of the Company's securities, not to sell, make any short sale of, loan, grant any option for the purchase of, or otherwise dispose of any Registrable Securities (other than those included in the registration) without the prior written consent of the Company or such underwriters, as the case may be, for such period of time (not to exceed [ ] days in the case of the Company's initial public offering) from the effective date of such registration as the Company and the underwriters may specify, so long as all Holders or stockholders holding more than one percent of the outstanding common stock and all officers and directors of the Company are bound by a comparable obligation provided, however, that nothing herein shall prevent any Holder that is a partnership or corporation from making a distribution of Registrable Securities to the partners or shareholders thereof that is otherwise in compliance with applicable securities laws, so long as such distributees agree to be so bound.

Section 12.   Information by Holder. The Holder or Holders of Registrable Securities included in any registration shall promptly furnish to the Company such information regarding such Holder or Holders and the distribution proposed by such Holder or Holders as the Company may request in writing and as shall be required in connection with any registration referred to herein.

Section 13.   Rule 144 and 144A Reporting. With a view to making available to Holders of Registrable Securities the benefits of certain rules and regulations of the SEC which may permit the sale of the Registrable Securities to the public without registration, the Company agrees at all times after ninety (90) days after the effective date of the first registration filed by the Company for an offering of its securities to the general public to:

         (a)   make and keep public information available, as those terms are understood and defined in Rule 144 and Rule 144A;

         (b)   use its best efforts to file with the Commission in a timely manner all reports and other documents required of the Company under the Securities Act and the Exchange Act;

      For purposes of facilitating sales pursuant to Rule 144A, so long as the Company is not subject to the reporting requirements of Section 13 or 15(d) of the Exchange Act, each Holder and any prospective purchaser of such Holder's securities shall have the right to obtain from the Company, upon request of the Holder prior to the time of sale, a brief statement of the nature of the business of the Company and the products and services it offers; and the Company's most recent balance sheet and profit and loss and retained earnings statements, and similar financial statements for the two preceding fiscal years (the financial statements should be audited to the extent reasonably available).

      Section 14.   Transfer of Registration Rights. The rights to cause the Company to register Registrable Securities of a Holder and keep information available granted to a Holder by the Company under Sections 5, 6, and 7, may be assigned by a Holder to any partner or shareholder of such Holder, to any other Holder, or to a transferee or assignee who receives at least 500,000 shares of Registrable Securities (as adjusted for stock splits and the like); provided, that the Company is given written notice by the Holder at the time of or within a reasonable time after said transfer, stating the name and address of said transferee or assignee and identifying the securities with respect to which such registration rights are being assigned.

      Section 15.   Limitations on Subsequent Registration Rights. From and after the date these registration rights are granted, the Company shall not, without the prior written consent of the Holders of not less than fifty percent (50%) of the Registrable Securities then held by Holders, enter into any agreement with any holder or prospective holder of any securities of the Company which would allow such holder or prospective holder to include such securities in any registration filed under Sections 5, 6 or 7 hereof other than rights identical or subordinate to the rights of any Holder hereunder.

Section 16.   Termination of Rights.

(a)   The rights of any particular Holder to cause the Company to register securities under Sections 5, 6 and 7 shall terminate with respect to such Holder at such time, following a bona fide, firmly underwritten public offering of shares of the Company's Common Stock registered under the Securities Act (provided that the aggregate gross offering price equals or exceeds $5,000,000), as such Holder is able to dispose of all of his Registrable Securities in one three-month (3-month) period pursuant to the provisions of Rule 144, provided that such Holder holds not more than 1% of the outstanding voting stock of the Company.

(b)   Notwithstanding the provisions of paragraph (a) of this Section 16, all rights of any particular Holder under this Agreement shall terminate at 5:00 p.m. Eastern time on the date seven (7) years after the closing date of the Company's first firmly underwritten public offering.

Section 17.   Remedies Upon Default or Delay.   (a) Without limitation of any other remedy available to a Holder under applicable law or otherwise, if the Company shall (1) fail to register Registrable Securities after it shall have been requested to do so by a Registrable Holder, or (2) fail to perform any of its obligations hereunder and as a result of such failure Holders have not been able to sell their Registrable Securities, or (3) act or fail to act in any manner such that one or more Holders have been delayed in the sale of their Registrable Securities, which delay is not expressly permitted by this Agreement, then any Holder adversely affected by such action, failure or delay shall be entitled to any or all of the following remedies, which may be elected in the sole discretion of such Holder:

(i)   Such Holder may otherwise sell its Registrable Securities and cause the Company to repurchase some or all of its Holder's Registrable Securities at a price equal to the Repurchase Price for each of such securities in accordance with paragraph (c) of this Section 17; or

(ii)   Such Holder may otherwise sell its Registrable Securities and cause the Company to pay to such Holder the amount of any Price Difference for any or all of such securities in accordance with paragraph (d) of this Section 17.

(a)   Repurchase of Securities.   Upon the occurrence of any of the events listed in paragraph (a) of this Section, a Holder may elect to cause the Company to repurchase any of such Holder's Registrable Securities by giving written notice to the Company. As soon as practicable (but not later than 10 days) thereafter the Company shall pay the Repurchase Price to the Holder for such repurchased securities; provided, however, that subject to paragraph (e) of this <u>Section 17</u>, if the Repurchase Price for any security shall not be immediately determinable, the Company and the Holder shall agree in good faith upon an estimate of the Repurchase Price for such security, which estimate shall be paid by the Company in accordance with this paragraph.

(b)   Payment of Price Difference. Upon the occurrence of any of the events listed in paragraph (a) of this <u>Section 17</u>, unless the Holder shall have been eligible to and have elected to cause the Company to repurchase such securities pursuant to paragraph (a) of this <u>Section 17</u>, the Holder may sell any security to any third party and the Company shall be obligated to pay to the Holder the amount of any Price Difference with respect to such security. If the Holder is unable to sell such security promptly pursuant to a registration statement, such Holder may sell such security in a manner and on such terms that the Holder in good faith believes are not unreasonable under the circumstances. The Company shall pay the Price Difference for each such security as soon as practicable (but not later than ten (10) days) after the Holder shall give written notice to the Company, which notice shall set forth the number and type of securities sold by such Holder and the Sale Dates and Selling Prices applicable thereto; provided, however, that, if the Price Difference for any security shall not be immediately determinable, the Company and the Holder shall agree in good faith upon an estimate of the Price Difference for such security, which estimate shall be paid by the Company in accordance with the terms of this paragraph.

(c)   Determination   of   Repurchase   Price   or   Price Difference. If the Repurchase Price or Price Difference for any security shall not be immediately determinable, the Company shall cooperate with any investment banking firm selected by the Holder and shall otherwise use its best efforts to cause such amount to be determined as quickly as possible. As soon as practicable after the final Repurchase Price or Price Difference shall have been determined, any difference between the final Repurchase Price or Price Difference and the estimated Repurchase Price or Price Difference, respectively, shall be paid by either the Company or the Holder to the other party, as the case may be, the amount of any underpayment being paid by the Company and the amount of any overpayment being paid by the Holder.

(d)   Effect of Laws Relating to Capital Impairment. If the Company shall be prevented by law from making any payment required to be made under this Section, the obligations hereunder shall be continuing obligations, and such payments shall be made in partial payments when, as soon as, and to the extent that, any portion of such payments shall later be permitted under applicable law. If more than one Holder has not been paid all amounts due as a result of the preceding sentence, all of such Holders shall share any partial payment on a pro rata basis based on the unpaid amount then owed to such Holders. No repurchase of any security shall be deemed to have been made, and the Holder shall continue to be deemed to be the owner of such security, until the date on which final payment of the Repurchase Price is made.

Section 18.   Representations and Warranties of the Company. The Company represents and warrants to the Holders as follows:

(a)   The execution, delivery and performance of this Agreement by the Company have been duly authorized by all requisite corporate action and will not violate any provision of law, any order of any court or other agency of government, the Articles of Organization or Bylaws of the Company or any provision of any indenture, agreement or other instrument to which it or any or its properties or assets is bound, conflict with, result in a breach of or constitute (with due notice or lapse of time or both) a default under any such indenture, agreement or other instrument or result in the creation or imposition of any lien, charge or encumbrance of any nature whatsoever upon any of the properties or assets of the Company.

(b)   This Agreement has been duly executed and delivered by the Company and constitutes the legal, valid and binding obligation of the Company, enforceable in accordance with its terms, subject to (i) applicable bankruptcy, insolvency, reorganization, fraudulent conveyance and moratorium laws and other laws of general application affecting enforcement of creditors' rights generally and (ii) the availability of equitable remedies as such remedies may be limited by equitable principles of general applicability (regardless of whether enforcement is sought in a proceeding in equity or at law).

Section 19.   Negative Covenant.

(a)   The Company may not, without the prior written consent of the Holders of at least two-thirds (2/3) of the then outstanding shares of Registrable Securities, grant any rights to any persons to register shares of capital stock or securities of the Company [unless such rights are, by their terms, substantially identical to the rights of the holders of Registrable Securities granted pursuant to this Agreement].

Section 20.   Miscellaneous.

(a)   Amendments. This Agreement may be amended only by a writing signed by the Holders of more than fifty percent (50%) of the Registrable Securities, as constituted from time to time. The Holders hereby consent to future amendments to this Agreement that permit future investors, other than employees, officers or directors of the Company, to be made parties hereto and to become Holders of Registrable Securities; provided, however, that no such future amendment may materially impair the rights of the Holders hereunder without obtaining the requisite consent of the Holders, as set forth above. For purposes of this Section, Registrable Securities held by the Company or beneficially owned by any officer or employee of the Company shall be disregarded and deemed not to be outstanding.

(b)   Counterparts. This Agreement may be executed in any number of counterparts, all of which shall constitute a single instrument.

(c)   Notices, Etc. All notices and other communications required or permitted hereunder shall be in writing and may be sent initially by facsimile transmission and shall be mailed by registered or certified mail, postage prepaid, or otherwise delivered by hand or by messenger, addressed (a) if to a Holder, at such Holder's address set forth on the books of the Company, or at such other address as such Holder shall have furnished to the Company in writing, or (b) if to any other holder of any Registrable Securities, at such address as such holder shall have furnished the Company in writing, or, until any such holder so furnishes an address to the Company, then to and at the address of the last holder of such securities who has so furnished an address to the Company, or (c) if to the Company, one copy should be sent to the Company's current address at [ ], or at such other address as the Company shall have furnished to the Holders. Each such notice or other communication shall for all purposes of this Agreement be treated as effective or having been given when delivered if delivered personally, or, if sent by first class, postage pre-paid mail, at the earlier of its receipt or seventy-two (72) hours after the same has been deposited in a regularly maintained receptacle for the deposit of the United States mail, addressed and mailed as aforesaid.

(d)   Non public information. Any other provisions of this agreement to the contrary notwithstanding, the Company's obligation to file a registration statement, or cause such registration statement to become and remain effective, shall be suspended for a period not to exceed thirty (30) days (and for periods not exceeding, in the aggregate, sixty (60) days in any twenty-four (24) month period) if there exists at the time material non-public information relating to the Company which, in the reasonable opinion of the Company, should not be disclosed.

(e)   Severability. If any provision of this Agreement shall be held to be illegal, invalid or unenforceable, such illegality, invalidity or unenforceability shall attach only to such provision and shall not in any manner affect or render illegal, invalid or unenforceable any other provision of this Agreement, and this Agreement shall be carried out as if any such illegal, invalid or unenforceable provision were not contained herein.

(f)   Dilution. If, and as often as, there is any change in the Common Stock or the Convertible Preferred Stock by way of a stock split, stock dividend, combination or reclassification, or through a merger, consolidation, reorganization or recapitalization, or by any other means, appropriate adjustment shall be made in the provisions hereof so that the rights and privileges granted hereby shall continue with respect to the Common Stock or the Convertible Preferred Stock as so changed.

(g)   Governing Law. This Agreement shall be governed by and construed under the laws of the State of [State] without regard to principles of conflict of law.

IN WITNESS WHEREOF, the parties hereto have executed this Agreement under seal as of the date first above written.

NEWCO, INC.

By_____
President

Stockholders:

_____

_____

_____

APPENDIX A

SOCIAL COVENANTS:

A SURVEY

OF THE INVESTMENT AGREEMENTS
OF

FIVE COMMUNITY DEVELOPMENT

VENTURE CAPITAL FUNDS

prepared for the
Community Development Venture Capital Alliance

by
David Ehrenfest Steinglass

August 1996

SOCIAL COVENANTS

1.   Introduction.

Community development venture capital ("CDVC") involves the imposition by a CDVC fund of a set of social, or non-financial, expectations on a portfolio company in consideration for the CDVC's investment. These expectations, often referred to as "social covenants," form the second of two bottom lines for CDVCs. Thus, while they expect to realize a quantifiable financial return on their investments (as does a mainstream investor), and they draft their documents to establish a set of incentives and enforcement mechanisms to insure that return, many CDVCs also expect some sort of measurable social return.

This report takes this principle as its starting point: that social returns, while not as easily quantified as financial returns, can and should be thought of as tangible outcomes. Thus, CDVCs should give as much thought to how to (and whether or not they should) include incentives and enforcement mechanisms in their agreements, in order to best insure the expected social returns.

This report includes a series of social covenants found in closing documents used by several CDVCs. These covenants are analyzed by the manner in which they define their expectations of social good and by the legal means through which those expectations are (a) imposed on porfolio companies and (b) enforced. Following this categorical analysis is a cataloguing of the various covenants, reproducing the language of each covenant and its documentary context in turn.

2.   The Use of Social Covenants.

The use of social covenants goes to the heart of the difference between "community development venture capital" and mainstream venture capital. The double bottom line implies an additional, non-financial return from CDVC investments; the use of social covenants, at least in theory, makes clear what the non-financial return is, and may also provide the CDVC a means to enforce its expectation of such a return. There are three, not unrelated reasons to consider refraining from the use of social covenants, or to at least consider using them in a guarded fashion. There are also good reasons to use them. These are considered briefly in turn.

The reasons not to use social covenants all relate to the far-from-settled principle that the different components of the double bottom line ("social" and "financial" returns) are at odds, and in fact can only be advanced one at the expense of the other. While the successes of the CDVC sector stand in stark contrast to that principle, it may remain an article of faith for at least two different audiences: future investors and disgruntled founders (and the courts in which they may challenge the actions of the CDVC). The first two reasons to hesitate in imposing social covenants on portfolio companies are (a) the possibility that non-financial priorities written into the organizational and investment documents of a portfolio company might frighten away later-stage investment and (b) the possibility that the founder of a portfolio company, having been fired or diluted in his or her ownership stake in the company, might sue the CDVC alleging that the social covenants impeded the effective (i.e., profitable) operation of the business.

These first two considerations lead to a third, which is that the stakes of *enforcing* social covenants, or even of exercising the power one bargains for as an investor (for example, taking control of the board if the performance of the company falls short of plan), may have to be raised to account for the possibility that an unhappy party might challenge such enforcement on the grounds that the covenants undermined the successful operation of the business. This is an argument an imaginative lawyer could make in telling a counter-factual story about later-stage investment that could not be lured to the table to provide needed capital <u>because</u> of the existence of social covenants, or a story about the limits the covenants imposed on the day-to-day operations of the company.

At least one of the surveyed funds has refrained for the most part from including social covenants in its investment documents. This fund, Northeast Ventures, prefers to assert its social goals through representation on the Board of Directors of each portfolio company, through reporting requirements, and through the role of its staff as mentors to the leaders of each company. The exception to this general principle for Northeast Ventures is a requirement that the portfolio company use Minnesota employment agencies as the first source for job referrals. The rationale that led Northeast Ventures away from more explicit social covenants is the concern about scaring off future investors. There is also a recognition that social covenants, absent a deeper commitment to the social values implicit in those covenants, are relatively valueless. Realizing that covenants are only as effective as the commitment of the portfolio company's owners to a set of shared social goals, and hoping that each company will attract more mainstream investments in the future, Northeast Ventures has taken a less overt approach to the enforcement of double bottom line expectations.

Reasons to impose some form of social covenant are connected to the differences between CDVC and mainstream venture capital, and begin with a challenge to the principle that profits and social return are inimical. The social change mission of the CDVC may in fact require an explicit statement of the purposes of the investment, and the underlying social content of those purposes. By making such a statement an integral part of a financing document, the CDVC makes clear its conviction that social goals must be viewed as vital aspirations of the portfolio company. Further, by making social covenants and their underlying aspirations an explicit part of the bargain, the CDVC may in fact stand on *firmer* ground when exercising its right to shape the course of the business. After all, if the Purchase Agreement clearly states that one of the reasons the CDVC is making its investment is to further job creation or other "non-financial" goals, it becomes more difficult for a party to that agreement to raise a challenge to the CDVC on the ground that it insisted on imposing social goals on an otherwise sound business, since those goals were part of what the CDVC paid for with its investment.

Funders of and investors in CDVCs may also expect to see an explicit and legally binding commitment to social goals in the financing documents accompanying the use of their money. Social covenants in this light do as much to advance the needs of the funder/investor for accountability on the part of the CDVC as they do to advance the social commitment and double bottom line of the portfolio company. On a similar note, social covenants accompanied by regular reporting covenants that specify some form of accounting for the achievement of social goals—for example, the number of temporary and permanent job placements achieved each month by a portfolio company operating a temporary agency—enable the CDVC to track the double bottom line, both for itself and for its funders/investors.

Conclusions drawn from the limited sample of financing documents are that a CDVC should carefully consider whether to include social covenants in its deals, why it is choosing (or choosing not) to do so, and the manner in which it does make explicit its expectations for a social return on its investments. It is to the last that this report now turns.

> ***Disclaimer:*** *The laws of each state vary, as does the enforceability of any given legal covenant or other term. Following is a general discussion of the various forms social covenants have taken in the financing documents of five community development venture capital funds. Before importing any of the general ideas in this discussion or any of the more specific language in the subsequent section into your documents, consult local counsel to determine whether those ideas or that language will be enforceable under the laws of the state (or states) that will govern your agreements.*

3. **Forms of Social Covenants; Remedies: A Categorical Analysis**

The social covenants surveyed in this report range from the broad to the specific. They are discussed here in two general categories: those that impose "aspirational" goals on the portfolio company without spelling out specific steps to be taken toward the realization of those goals and those that impose detailed obligations on the portfolio company and others.

Following the discussion of the covenants themselves is a brief analysis of the range of enforcement mechanisms used to give "teeth" to the covenants. Finally, the next section of the report extracts language from the five sets of closing documents made available for this report.

3.1.   *The Social Covenants*

Examples of "aspirational" covenants include the requirement that the work of the company (and thus the jobs created) must be located in the CDVC's home state. An alternative, somewhat more targeted covenant simultaneously requires the company to create "good quality" jobs (not defined beyond that) for "disadvantaged workers" (a term that is defined by example). This second covenant is in some ways less specific than the first, as it does not impose a geographic restriction on the company. It does go further, however, in articulating the CDVC's expectations. In addition, the covenant refers to language in the "Summary Data" section of the Investment and Shareholder Agreement, itself phrased to explicitly make the targeted job creation goals part of the consideration the CDVC expects to realize in return for its money— effectively wedding the double bottom lines. This effect is further reinforced by information requirements that include monthly statements from the company of the number of temporary and permanent job placements, coupled with more traditional financial reporting.*

A more specific covenant is one that requires the portfolio company to use state employment agencies as the first source for referrals in all hiring. This requirement is very specific, and presumably verifiable as far as it goes. However, it does not require anything more of the company than that it solicit referrals from state agencies—actual hiring decisions are outside the scope of the covenant. However, and this is taken up below, the CDVC retains a significant voice on the Board of the company, constant visitation rights, and the ability to assume control of the Board if this, or any other, covenant is violated. These additional elements lend the covenant more force.

---

* These requirements also have a "financial" character. The portfolio company is a temporary services company, the "sales" of which are temporary and permanent job placements. Further, the information requirement regarding job placements does not include information about the income level or other characteristics of the job recipients, nor of the "quality" of the jobs.

Another specific covenant mandates the creation of an employee stock ownership plan. To the extent that employee ownership in turn increases job quality, this covenant can be read as requiring a commitment to the larger goal of "quality job" creation and to increasing community wealth. The covenant is not backed up by remedies, however, and on the face of the agreement, if the covenant is violated that violation does not constitute an event of default. The CDVC does retain the shares of portfolio company stock reserved for the plan; in the event that the plan is never adopted, the CDVC and not the founders, retains the stock, which to some extent may diminish the incentive on the part of the founders to delay or avoid compliance with the covenant.

The most specific set of social covenants appears in the form of a side agreement between the CDVC, the portfolio company and a group of job training agencies, for the provision and utilization of job training and referral services. The Employment Training Agreement sets forth the particular obligations of each party. The obligations of the company include: (a) hiring quotas, specifying the income level of at least some of the new hires; (b) commitments to maintain a workforce a certain percentage of which was referred by one of the training programs; (c) provide to those targeted employees the standard company benefits package; (d) notify the CDVC of new positions; and (e) assist the CDVC and the other parties to the Agreement in tracking and reporting progress in hiring trainees. The Agreement is a closing document, although it is not referenced in the other documents. However, the CDVC retains a seat on the Board of Directors, enabling it to monitor the company's performance under the Agreement.

The next section, a discussion of remedies, considers more fully how social covenants can be and are enforced.

3.2.   Remedies

Enforcement of social covenants (or any other form of covenant) takes several forms. Some agreements provide for information rights and a minority position on the Board of Directors of a portfolio company. These rights exist whether or not the covenants are complied with; the philosophy underlying informational covenants is that by virtue of a presence on the Board, the CDVC can influence the direction of the company and encourage good behavior. A variant on this theme provides the CDVC with an exit opportunity after a certain number of years (from this limited sample, five years after the initial investment appears to be standard); this exit can be used as a last resort in the event the company is falling short of the CDVC's social goals. Exit on these terms often comes at a financial cost to the CDVC. Another approach is to define "events of default" and then provide for a set of enhanced rights on the part of the CDVC until such time as the default has been "cured." Yet a fourth form of enforcement mechanism—involving the Golden Rule—is the benchmarked, or staged, investment. The CDVC invests money in stages, at the end of each of which the progress of the company towards meeting its business (and social) goals can be reevaluated by the CDVC as part of the decision to undertake the next investment.[*]

The five agreements examined for this report, and excerpted below, span the range of these options. If the four general categories outlined in the preceding paragraph are listed in increasing order of strength, the CDVC agreements tend to use the less strong remedies.

One agreement provides for a two-stage investment; however, the stages are relatively proximate in time, and the second investment decision may occur too early in the company's life to be able to make fulfillment of social covenants a major part of the decision.

Another agreement, excerpted at length below, sets up a control flip in the event of default, and includes the breach of its social covenant in the definition of an event of default. Pursuant to the terms of the control flip, the CDVC is entitled to elect a majority of the Board of Directors, and once in control of the company, to revise the business plan of the company or arrange for, and approve, its sale.[*]

---

[*] In order to avoid challenge as a result of the decision to <u>not</u> invest in a later round of a benchmarked deal, if that decision is driven by disappointment in the company's commitment to social goals, a CDVC would be well-advised to make explicit in the initial investment documents that part of the reason for making the investment is to advance social goals. This effectively makes the social goals part of the measurement of progress against the benchmark.   See BCLF Ventures excerpt, below.   Staged investments, while complicated to negotiate and structure, have become increasingly popular among traditional venture capitalists, as they guarantee the VC a measure of control (as long as the company continues to need outside investment), and because they provide a good mechanism for "splitting the difference" in disputes over valuation and pricing.   For example, a founder's projections, rosy though they may be, can be used to set the floor in terms of the share in the company the VC will accept (if the company has profits of x, the VC gets 25% of the company); the VC's guess at the future can set the ceiling (if the company has profits of $0.5x$, the VC gets 75% of the company).

[*] This term is a good example of the type of provision that may be enforceable in some states and not in others. Some states may require an affirmative vote of the holders of two-thirds of the voting stock of the company in order to approve a sale of all or substantially all of the assets of the company, despite contractual terms to the contrary. A variant on this term, which may be enforceable in Delaware, is a term providing for "drag-along" rights, enabling a minority group of shareholders to force the sale of the company's stock by all the shareholders. See <u>Shields v. Shields</u>, 498 A.2d 161, 168 (Del. Ch. 1985) (affirming, albeit in dictum, enforceability of "drag-along" rights); see also Joseph W. Bartlett, Equity Finance § 10.15 (1995).

Several of the agreements include provisions enabling the CDVC to recoup its investment, at some discount, either after a period of time or in one instance, upon breach of any covenants in the investment agreement. The latter provision appears in a royalty agreement, and accelerates repayment of the company's debt obligation under that agreement. This is somewhat different than a forced repayment of equity, as the company will not be restrained by state corporation laws that can limit the ability of a company to cash out equity investors if that process will too deeply cut into the company's net worth. By contrast, acceleration of debt payments, while still working havoc on the company's balance sheet, will not be impeded by those laws. (However, restrictions still may apply to debt repayment; again, consult local counsel.) The agreements that provide for an exit for the CDVC in the form of an equity payout each preclude exit for a period of years, and then take one of two forms: either (a) a "put" option under which the CDVC redeems its stock for cash and/or a promissory note of the company at a pre-arranged price or (b) demand registration rights. These empower the CDVC to force the company to register the shares of stock held by the CDVC and to sell those shares on the public market. This right can have limited use in practice, but may be helpful in convincing a reluctant founder to change the way the company operates.

Finally, each of the agreements provides for some form of information rights coupled, in three of five agreements, with Board representation. The language of the three agreements that do provide for Board representation varies; some go into greater detail about the number of Board seats and how they are filled than others, which merely reserve a single Board seat for the CDVC as long as it holds shares of stock in the portfolio company. The advantage to the latter approach is that it guarantees the CDVC information and a voice in the running of the company without incurring the potential liability that Board control can lead to, particularly when Board control is held by a minority shareholder. At least one such provision sets Board representation for the CDVC at a majority of the Board so long as the CDVC holds at least 40% of the voting stock of the company. Once the CDVC's interest drops below 40%, its position on the Board declines to a minority stake, until the stockholdings are less than 20%, at which point the Board representation for the CDVC equals its percentage stake in the company's voting stock.

4. *Social Covenants: Excerpts From Agreements*

CDVC	Ben Franklin Technology Center of Southeastern Pennsylvania
Agreement	Emerging Company Investment Funding Agreement

6.0 COMPANY RESPONSIBILITIES

* * *

6.03 Commonwealth Activities. The Company will perform research and development activities in connection with the Project Plan at facilities located in Pennsylvania. For a period of five years following the end of Ben Franklin funding, product development and manufacturing activity deriving from the activities funded under this Agreement will be located within Pennsylvania unless otherwise specifically approved in writing by the Center.

8. EVENT OF DEFAULT
Any of the following shall constitute an event of default ("Event of Default"):

* * *

8.02 If the Company fails to comply with any of its responsibilities or obligations under this Agreement (other than as provided in Section 8.01), and such failure shall continue uncured for fifteen (15) days after the date (a) the Center gives notice of such failure to the Company, or (b) the Company notifies the Center of such failure as required by Section 6.12, whichever occurs first.

Remedy	acceleration with a prepayment penalty

9. REMEDIES

If an Event of Default occurs, without taking further action, the Center shall have the right to treat an amount equal to the prepayment amount as set forth on Exhibit C as immediately due and payable (regardless of whether the Company is otherwise obligated to make payments to the Center under this Agreement), and the Center shall have the right to exercise any remedy provided in this Agreement or under applicable law. All expenses and costs incurred by the Center in enforcing this Agreement shall be paid by the Company.

CDVC: BCLF Ventures
Agreement: Investment and Shareholder Agreement

Summary of Basic Data

1.20 Community Impact Goals: All parties to this Agreement acknowledge and understand that Purchasers are vitally interested in the Company's activities having a positive impact on local communities, and that but for the commitment of the Company, the Founder and the Company's other senior management to, and the Company's prospects for, having a positive impact on low-income and/or other disadvantaged populations, the Purchasers would not enter into this Agreement. Accordingly, as a material inducement for Purchasers' agreement to make the investments in the Company contemplated by the Investment Documents, the Founder and the Company hereby commit to pursue the Company's business plan in such fashion as to achieve such positive impacts; by way of example and not limitation, the Company and Purchasers anticipate that the Company will achieve social goals such as the following:

    (a)   to create good quality, long-term temporary and "temp to perm" jobs for disadvantaged workers, among whom may be legal immigrants, people currently receiving welfare, graduates of substance abuse programs, low-income urban youth, or handicapped individuals.

    (b)   to provide on-going training and/or counseling support to employees making the transition into the "mainstream" work force.

(c) to coordinate on-the-job peer support by means of a team-based approach; the Company's team leaders will play a central role in overseeing on-site work, and providing managerial continuity and peer support.

Certain Covenants of the Company
7.4 Community Impact Goals. The Company shall use its best efforts to achieve the Community Impact Goals specified in Section 1.20.

Remedy: The investment is made in three stages (of which BCLF Ventures is a participant in the latter two)— BCLF Ventures thus retains the right not to invest in the third round (thus invoking the Golden Rule: "He who has the gold makes the rules")

Other rights:	Observation rights (see below), board representation (3 of 7 seats), monthly reports on temporary and permanent job placements (in addition to financial reporting on monthly, quarterly and annual bases)

Certain Covenants of the Company

7.15 Observation Rights. In addition to the Purchasers' Board Rights, the Company shall permit the Purchasers, or authorized representatives of the Purchasers, to attend, at their own expense, all meetings of the Board of Directors of the company, and of any other committee or group exercising responsibilities comparable to those exercised by the Board of Directors, as non-participating observers of such meetings. The Company shall give each Purchaser such notice of any such meeting as shall be given to members of the Board of Directors or committees thereof.

> **CDVC:** Northeast Ventures
> **Agreements:** Stock Purchase Agreement; Articles of Incorporation (voting, remedy); Nomination Agreement (voting)

11.17   Employment Practices. The Company agrees to utilize the services of appropriate State of Minnesota agencies as the first referral source in all hirings.

> **Remedy:** violation of any covenant is an event of default; triggers control flip—Northeast Ventures elects a majority of board, can force sale of company

DEFAULT

13.1   Events of Default. The following shall be deemed to be Events of Default for purposes of this Agreement:

* * *

(d)   if default shall be made in the due and punctual performance or observance of any term contained in this Agreement or the Company shall violate any of the negative covenants set forth in Section 10 of this Agreement, and such default or violation shall have continued for a period of 15 days after written notice thereof to the Company by the holder of any Shares; provided, however, that the rights and obligations set forth in Sections 11, 12, and 13 shall terminate and no Event of Default shall occur or continue after there has been a sale to the public of Common Stock of the Company in an underwritten public offering registered pursuant to a registration statement on Form S-1 (or any successor form) by the Company of its Common Stock in which the aggregate gross proceeds to the Company are at least Five Million Dollars ($5,000,000.00) and the public offering price is not less than Ten Dollars ($10.00) per share (as adjusted from time to time upon the occurrence of any subdivision, stock split, combination or change of Common Stock into a different number of shares of the same or any other class or classes of shares).

13.2   Remedy Upon Events of Default. Upon the occurrence of an Event of Default as herein defined, and so long as such Event of Default continues unremedied, then, unless such Event of Default shall have been waived in the manner provided in Section 13.1 hereof, the holders of the Preferred Stock shall be entitled to elect a majority of the Board of Directors in the manner provided in the Articles.

That new Board of Directors may, in addition to all other action taken by the Board of Directors pursuant to the laws of the State of Minnesota, the Articles and Bylaws of the Company:

(a)   sell or otherwise dispose of all or substantially all of the assets of the Company and wind up the affairs of the Company; or

(b)   adopt a new business plan including the change of purpose and objectives of the Company and pursue such business plan.

Articles of Incorporation (Amended)

3.4   <u>Voting Rights; Board of Directors</u>.   The holders of the Series A Preferred Stock shall be entitled to notice of and to attend all meetings of the shareholders of the corporation and shall be entitled to the number of votes for each share held equal to the number of shares of Common Stock into which such share of Series A Preferred Stock is then convertible pursuant to Section 3.7 hereof. So long as the holders of the Series A Preferred Stock hold forty percent (40%) or more of the aggregate voting rights of the Series A Preferred Stock and Common Stock, the holders of the Series A Preferred Stock shall be entitled to elect that number of directors that is the lowest number that constitutes a majority of the members of the Board of Directors, and the holders of the Common Stock shall be entitled to elect the remaining members of the Board of Directors. So long as the holders of the Series A Preferred Stock hold twenty percent (20%) or more of the aggregate voting rights of the Series A Preferred Stock and Common Stock, the holders of the Series A Preferred Stock shall have the right to elect a number of members of the Board of Directors that is one person less than a majority, and the remaining directors shall be elected by the holders of Series A Preferred Stock and Common Stock voting together. Except as otherwise provided in this Section 3.4 or in Section 3.5, or as required under the Minnesota Business Corporation Act, the holders of Series A Preferred Stock and Common Stock shall vote together as a single class.

The procedures for electing directors pursuant to this subsection 3.4 are set forth in subsection 3.5(3).

3.5   <u>Special Voting Rights</u>.

(1)   <u>Protective Provisions</u>. Without the affirmative vote or consent of holders of at least a majority of the Series A Preferred Stock at the time outstanding, voting separately as a class, the corporation shall not:

(a)   Authorize or issue any (i) additional Series A Preferred Stock or (ii) shares of stock having priority over Series A Preferred Stock or ranking on a parity therewith as to the payment of dividends or as to the payment or distribution of assets upon the liquidation or dissolution, voluntary or involuntary, of the corporation; or

(b)   Declare or pay any dividend or make any other distribution on any shares of capital stock of the corporation at any time created and issued ranking junior to Series A Preferred Stock with respect to the right to receive dividends and the right to the distribution of assets upon liquidation, dissolution or winding up of the corporation (hereinafter called "Junior Stock"), other than dividends or distributions payable solely in shares of Junior Stock, or purchase, redeem or otherwise acquire for any consideration (other than in exchange for or out of the net cash proceeds of the contemporaneous issue or sale of other shares of Junior Stock), or set aside as a sinking fund or other fund for the redemption or repurchase of any shares of Junior Stock or any warrants, rights or options to purchase shares of Junior Stock, except as specifically permitted by the terms of the Stock Purchase Agreement;

(c)   Amend the articles of incorporation of the corporation so as to adversely affect any of the rights, preferences or privileges of the holders of Series A Preferred Stock; or

(d)   Sell, lease, license or otherwise dispose of all or substantially all of its assets, or consolidate with or merge into any other corporation or entity, or permit any other corporation or entity to consolidate or merge into it, except that any subsidiary of the corporation may merge into another subsidiary or into the corporation.

(2)   <u>Event of Default</u>.   Upon the occurrence of an Event of Default, as that term is defined in the Purchase Agreement, the holders of Series A Preferred Stock shall be entitled to elect that number of directors that is the lowest number that constitutes a majority of the members of the Board of Directors, and the holders of Common Stock shall be entitled to elect the remaining members of the Board of Directors. The right of the holders of Series A Preferred Stock to vote as provided in this subsection 3.5(2) shall cease upon the curing of the Event of Default which gave rise to such right and the curing of all Events of Default occurring after the Event of Default which gave rise to such right.

(3)   <u>Special Election Procedures</u>.   At any time after the right to elect a majority of the members of the Board of Directors shall have become vested in the holders of Series A Preferred Stock as provided in subsection 3.5(2) or subsection 3.4, the secretary of the corporation may, and upon the request of the record holders of at least twenty percent (20%) of the outstanding shares of Series A Preferred Stock addressed to the secretary at the

principal executive office of the corporation shall call a meeting for the election of directors, to be held at the place and upon the notice provided in the bylaws of the corporation for the holding of a regular meeting. If such meeting shall not be so called within ten (10) days after personal service of the request, or within fifteen (15) days after mailing of the same by registered mail within the United States of America, then a person designated by the record holders of at least 20% of the outstanding shares of Series A Preferred Stock may call such meeting at the place and upon the notice above provided and for that purpose shall have the right, during regular business hours, to examine and to make copies of extracts of the stock records of the corporation. At any meeting so called or at any regular meeting held while the holders of the Series A Preferred Stock have the right to elect a majority of the members of the Board of Directors as provided in subsection 3.5(2) or subsection 3.4, the holders of a majority of the then-outstanding shares of Series A Preferred Stock, present in person or by proxy, shall be sufficient to constitute a quorum for the election of directors as herein provided. The terms of office of all persons who are directors of the corporation at the time of such meeting shall terminate upon the election at such meeting by the holders of the Series A Preferred Stock of the number of directors they are entitled to elect and the persons so elected as directors by the holders of Series A Preferred Stock, together with such persons, if any, as may be elected directors by the holders of Common Stock, shall constitute the duly elected directors of the corporation. In the event the holders of Common Stock fail to elect any of the directors which they are entitled to elect at such meeting, additional directors may be appointed by the directors elected by the holders of Series A Preferred Stock. If, during any interval between regular meetings of shareholders while the holders of Series A Preferred Stock are entitled to elect a majority of the Board of Directors after the initial election by such holders has been made, the number of directors who have been elected by the holders of Series A Preferred Stock or the holders of Common Stock, as the case may be, shall, by reason of resignation, death or removal, be less than the total number of directors subject to election by all such holders, any vacancy in directors elected by the holders of Common Stock shall be filled by a majority vote of the remaining directors then in office who were elected by the holders of Common Stock or succeeded a director so elected, although such majority be less than a quorum, and any vacancy in the directors elected by the holders of Series A Preferred Stock shall be filled by a majority of the remaining directors then in office who were elected by the holders of Series A Preferred Stock or succeeded a director so elected, although such majority may be less than a quorum.

Whenever the voting rights of Series A Preferred Stock shall cease as provided in subsection 3.5(2), the Board of Directors shall call a meeting of shareholders at which all directors will be elected as provided in subsection 3.4 above and the term of office of all persons who are then directors of the corporation shall terminate immediately upon the election of their successors.

Nomination Agreement

THE UNDERSIGNED, consisting of the Company, the Founding Shareholders, and the Option Holders (as those terms are defined in the Purchase Agreement referred to below), as required by Section 11.4 of the Purchase Agreement For Series A Convertible 8% Cumulative Preferred Stock (the "Purchase Agreement"), do separately agree as follows:

WE HEREBY AGREE, that in submitting to the Company's Shareholders and Board of Directors the names of nominees for election as directors or in filing interim vacancies, we will use our best efforts to cause any person nominated by the Purchasers (as that term is defined in the Purchase Agreement) to be elected as a Purchaser's Director.

COMPANY NAME

By: _____

Its President

_____
Shareholder name

_____
Shareholder name

Other rights:	Board representation (see above "Voting Rights; Board of Directors" in Articles, also Stock Purchase Agreement, below), observation rights (see below), financial reporting on monthly, quarterly and annual bases; "put" after five years

Stock Purchase Agreement
Covenants of the Company

11.4   Representation on Board of Directors. The Company shall take such actions as may be necessary to maintain a Board of Directors that initially shall consist of five (5) persons but shall in no event exceed seven (7) persons. The Articles shall provide that so long as the holders of record of outstanding Preferred Stock issued pursuant to this Agreement (giving effect to conversion pursuant to the Articles) represent forty percent (40%) or more of the voting rights of the Capital Stock of the Company, the holders of the Preferred Stock shall have the right to elect the majority of the Board of Directors.

The Articles shall further provide that so long as the holders of record of outstanding Preferred Stock issued pursuant to this Agreement (giving effect to conversion pursuant to the Articles) represent twenty percent (20%) or more of the voting rights of the Capital Stock of the Company, but less than forty percent (40%) of such rights, such holders shall have the right to elect two (2) members of the Board of Directors. The directors which the Purchasers are entitled to elect pursuant to this Section 11.4 shall be known as the "Purchasers' Directors". In the event the Board of Directors is expanded to seven (7) directors, the number of directors which are Purchasers' Directors shall also be expanded to three (3) directors so as to assure the Purchasers continued representation upon the Board of Directors. In the event of the death, resignation or removal of any Purchasers' Directors, the Purchaser shall be entitled to nominate such Director's successor. The Company by this Agreement, and the Founding Shareholders and Option Holders by separate agreement, have agreed that in submitting to the Company's stockholders or Board of Directors the names of nominees for election as directors or in filling interim vacancies, they will use their best efforts to cause any person nominated by the Purchasers to be elected as a Purchasers' Director.

Nomination of Purchasers' Directors shall be made in a writing signed by Purchasers holding a majority of the Preferred Stock.

Any determination by the Company to exercise the Call Option described in Article 5 hereof shall be made by a majority of the directors of the Company who are not Purchaser's Directors.

11.5   Inspection and Attendance. So long as the Purchasers collectively hold of record twenty percent (20%) or more of the issued and outstanding Capital Stock, the Company will permit the Purchaser Representative and any of its partners, officers or employees, or any outside representatives designated by such Purchaser Representative and reasonably satisfactory to the Company, to attend meetings of the Board of Directors as an observer and to visit and inspect at the expense of such Purchaser Representative, except for any expenses required to be borne by the Company under Minnesota Statutes, Section 302A, 461, as now in effect or hereafter amended or succeeded, any of the properties of the Company or its subsidiaries, including their books and records (and to make photocopies thereof or extracts therefrom), and to discuss their affairs, finances and accounts with their officers, except with respect to trade secrets and similar confidential information, all to such reasonable extent and at such reasonable times and intervals as such Purchaser Representative may reasonably request without disruption of the Company's operations.

CDVC:	CEI Ventures
Agreement:	Employment Training Agreement; Stock Purchase Agreement; Articles, Shareholder Agreement (Remedy); Registration Rights Agreement

Employment and Training Agreement
CEI Ventures has a detailed Employment and Training Agreement that is a closing document, yet is not referenced in the other closing documents. It is thus not enforceable by means of rights created by those other documents, but merely on its own terms. Despite the peripheral nature of this agreement, CEI Ventures has been very successful by all accounts in making investments that further the social goals of their fund.

Other rights:	Board representation (Shareholders Agreement, see below, Articles); information rights; "put" (see below) and demand registration rights after five years (see Registration Rights Agreement, below); protection as a minority shareholder (see below)

Stock Purchase Agreement
IV. INFORMATION
4.1   Access to Information. Purchaser and its representatives shall have the right to visit and inspect any of the properties of the Company and shall have full access to the financial and business records of the Company, including the company's customer and supplier lists, and to the assets, and the Company shall furnish Purchaser or its representatives with all information that Purchaser may reasonably require with regard to the Business and the operations and affairs generally of the Company. The exercise of such right to access and inspection by or on behalf of Purchaser shall not affect or mitigate the covenants, representations and warranties of the Company under this Agreement. The rights set forth in this paragraph shall be exercised solely in furtherance of proper interests of a shareholder.
Shareholders Agreement
Section 9. Special Put Right Respecting Preferred Stock.

(a)   The options granted under Section 3 shall not apply to any purchase or sale made pursuant to the terms and provisions of Section 9, and the parties to this Agreement may exercise the options granted in Section 9 even if such exercise is inconsistent with the terms and provisions of Section 3 of this Agreement.

(b)   The Company and the Shareholders hereby grant to CEI the right and option (herein called the "Put Option") to cause the Company to redeem, on the terms and conditions herein provided, the shares of Preferred Stock or the shares of Common Stock into which such shares have been converted owned by CEI (the "Put Shares"). On or after February 22, [1999—*5 yrs after closing*], on one or more occasions, CEI may cause the Company to redeem all or any part of the Put Shares by delivering a written notice to the Company. The Redemption Price per share for the Put Shares shall be based on valuation of the Company determined by multiplying the average annual net income after taxes for the preceding two fiscal years by six, and then dividing such number by the number of shares of Common Stock then outstanding. For purposes of determining the Redemption Price, the Preferred Stock shall be deemed to have been converted into Common Stock at the Conversion Ratio then in effect, and such shares shall be deemed to be outstanding. The Redemption Price for the Put Shares shall be the Redemption Price per share, multiplied by the number of shares of Common Stock into which such Preferred Stock could have been converted on the date of redemption. The Company shall have the right to designate a purchaser for the Put Shares on the same terms as set forth in Section 6.

(c)   Within 30 days after exercise of the Put Option, CEI shall deliver to the Company at the address provided in Section 13 certificates representing the shares being sold, duly endorsed in blank or with blank stock powers attached, with signatures guaranteed by a commercial bank or trust company or a member firm of a national securities exchange if requested, and with all requisite stock transfer tax stamps attached or provided for. Upon receipt of such certificates, the Company shall promptly deliver to CEI at the address provided in Section 13 a note for the Redemption Price for the Put Shares, payable over five years in monthly payments and bearing interest at the rate of 10% per year.

(d) Notwithstanding any other provision herein contained to the contrary, the Company shall not be obligated to redeem the Put Shares if (i) the Company is unable to obtain the consent of its bank or institutional lender, to the extent required by the financing agreements with such creditor, or (ii) the Maine Business Corporation Law restricts or prohibits such redemption because the Company's assets remaining after such redemption or the Company's surplus account is legally insufficient. The Company's obligations under this Section 9 shall automatically be reinstated upon the satisfaction of either of the events set forth in (i) or (ii) above.

Registration Rights Agreement

(b)   Demand Registration. At any time after February 22, [1999— *5 yrs after closing*], or after an initial public offering before such date, the Holder, with the consent of holders of no less than 2/3 of the then outstanding Preferred Stock and Investor Stock, may request the Company to effect the registration of the Investor Stock by giving the Company notice in writing. The Company shall promptly give written notice of such proposed registration to the Purchaser and all Permitted Transferees who are holders of Investor Stock. The Company shall promptly use its best efforts to effect the registration under the Securities Act of 1933, as amended, of the shares of the Investor Stock specified in the Holder's notice and in any response received from the Purchaser and Permitted Transferees within 30 days after the written notice from the Company (the "Registration Shares"). The Company shall not be obligated to effect any registration, however, except in accordance with the following provisions:

(i)   The Company shall not be required to file more than one registration statement registering the Investor Stock under the paragraph (b), or any registration statement within six months after the effective date of any previous registration statements by the Company with the Securities and Exchange Commission. If the Investor Stock is withdrawn from registration or an offering is deregistered at the request of the Holder, the Company's obligation to effect one registration shall be deemed satisfied unless the holder of the withdrawn shares shall reimburse the Company for such holder's pro rata portion of all expenses payable by the Company in connection with the preparation and filing of such registration statement.

(ii)   The Company shall not be obligated to effect any registration unless the aggregate gross public offering price of all shares of common stock to be sold under such registration shall be at least equal to $2,000,000.

(iii)   The Company may include in any registration requested under this paragraph (b) any authorized but unissued shares of common stock for sale by the Company (the "Corporate Shares") or any issued and outstanding shares of Common Stock for sale by other shareholders (the "Secondary Shares"), provided that such inclusion does not prevent the entire number of Registration Shares from being included in the registration. If the underwriter determines that marketing factors require a limitation of the number of shares to be registered, then the number of shares otherwise to be included shall be limited as follows: the number of shares to be included in the offering shall be reduced first, by reducing the Secondary Shares pro rata among such shareholders, and second, by reducing the Corporate Shares to be included, and those shares excluded shall be withheld from the market by the Company or such other shareholders for a period to be determined by the managing underwriter.

(c)   <u>Expenses</u>.   All expenses incurred in connection with any registration, qualification or compliance pursuant to this Agreement shall be borne by the Company, provided, however that the Company shall not be required to pay fees of legal counsel of the Holder or underwriters' fees, discounts, or commissions relating to Registration Shares.

CDVC:	CARESBAC (Polish fund of Small Enterprise Assistance Funds)
Agreement:	Investment Agreement

10. **Employee Stock Option Plan.** Principal, Principal's Spouse and CARESBAC recognize the importance of motivating and retaining key Polish employees of Investee. Accordingly, the foregoing parties agree to develop, within one hundred eighty (180) days after the Closing Date an employee stock option plan which will seek to achieve the foregoing objectives through the making available for purchase by such employees some or all of the Reserved Shares. Such plan will be administered by Investee's Supervisory Board, acting on the recommendations of the Management Board. The price of such shares to the selected employees shall be the price, in US dollar equivalent terms, at which such Reserved Shares were issued CARESBAC plus interest compounded at a rate equal to the United States prime rate (as listed in *The Wall Street Journal* on the date of sale, and defined as the base rate on corporate loans posted by at least 75% of the nation's [the United States] 30 largest banks) plus seven hundred (700) basis points.

Remedy:	CARESBAC retains control of the shares reserved for the employee stock option plan until the plan is created, at which time CARESBAC will transfer the shares.

David Ehrenfest Steinglass

David Ehrenfest Steinglass received his A.B. *magna cum laude* in Urban Studies from Harvard College in 1989 and spent four years working in the community development field before entering New York University School of Law. He received his J.D. *magna cum laude* in 1996. Following law school, he clerked for the Honorable Leonard B. Sand, United States District Judge, Southern District of New York for the 1996-1997 Term.

David spent his summers during law school learning about the legal aspects of the private equity business at Wilson, Sonsini, Goodrich & Rosati in Palo Alto, California; Foley, Hoag & Eliot in Boston, Massachusetts; and with Joe Bartlett at Morrison & Foerster LLP in New York City.